YOU

YOU

A Guide to Deeper Connection, a
Lifestyle of Ease, and Massive Results

Brandon Hawk

HAWK HOUSE

YOU

A Guide to Deeper Connection, a Lifestyle of Ease, and Massive Results

ISBN 978-1-5445-0141-3 *Paperback*

978-1-5445-0140-6 *Ebook*

978-1-5445-0142-0 *Audiobook*

This book is dedicated to my family. To my wife, Ginny, and my kids. And to my larger family—my mom and dad, brothers and sisters—who have journeyed through this process together, who have risked everything for connection. Thank you for being so brave.

Contents

Introduction

You're lying there awake, once again, at 2 a.m. You have a great life, so why do you feel so alone, so disconnected from yourself and others?

Why are you running scared?

All you know is that you feel a great divide, a disconnect of sorts between you and the person lying next to you. You're not getting what you want out of the relationship. You want to escape when your kids are around but miss them deeply when you're gone. Why can't you be present?

You worry about the future, too. You feel a great sense of unfulfilled potential, but how could you fully show up and share what you feel? You have too much riding on that kind of honesty. You have a great life, remember?

No, you just can't be that real. So you self-medicate. You find ways to escape—through work, wine, or otherwise. And now you feel guilt and shame for what you do in secret (and for what you don't do for that matter).

This is the disconnected life, and I know exactly where you are.

YOU'RE NOT ALONE

For the past fifteen years, I have been my own primary guinea pig. I have lived out what I teach. I get paid multiple six figures to teach high achievers my process—the process of becoming an expert at YOU.

This process requires honesty. There's so much going off inside of you, and it's time to get real about what's going on.

I feel you. I hear you. I see you. You're going through a lot. What you're enduring internally—and externally—is not okay.

But I also want you to know I'm not scared of where you are. I repeat: I'm not scared of your questions, your disconnected thoughts, your fear, and escape mechanisms. All I ask is that you stop denying what is really going on.

Stop denying that your life is full of responsibility without nurture. Duty without passion. Guilt without freedom. Stop.

Because you know the truth: things are already breaking inside of you, no matter how skilled you are at covering it all up. This dis-ease in you is festering in the cracks and crevices of the armor you've built around yourself. The dis-ease could be showing itself in the form of weight gain, a short fuse with your family, or your habit of escaping into your phone.

It's time to say *enough is enough*. It's time to reconnect back to YOU.

Why does this matter? Because your life is meant for more. You are not meant to feel constantly separated, alone, left out, disconnected from your heart, passionless, and bored.

No, you are meant for so much more.

After more than ten thousand hours of coaching, I have seen this process work time and time again. I have seen lives transformed. Yours can be transformed, too. Together, YOU can do this.

The subtitle of this book is not a marketing tactic. If you move through this process with me, you will experience deeper connection and a lifestyle of ease, while creating massive results. I don't think you heard me: I'm talking about wild monkey sex with your partner, living in places where people typically only vacation, and your mailbox is loading up with cash!

Are you ready?

MY STORY

In this book, I share many moments of my story. I grew up with amazing parents in an environment in which I could thrive externally, but the programming I received left me feeling desperately alone.

I found out that I was affirmed and acknowledged when I performed. So I did. I got so good at performing that I became a professional tennis player and ended up accomplishing my boyhood dream of playing in Wimbledon at the age of twenty-two. This, along with other amazing moments in my athletic career, were unforgettable, but they also revealed to me just how disconnected I truly felt.

From seventeen to twenty-two, I had the experience most people have in their fifties, and I realized none of it was going to complete me.

I ended my tennis career and went searching for the connection I lacked. In reality, I was stumbling in the dark. I had no roadmap, only a sense that there must be a better way. So I headed home and started asking questions.

This choice led to a humbling drop-off; I went from playing sports professionally to working in my dad's manufacturing business. My energy had to go somewhere, so I put it into growing the family business. We're talking exponential growth—the 500 percent kind.

During this time, I also became a senior pastor and launched a school of transformation at the church. By my mid-twenties, I once again had outward success, but my internal world was now deconstructing. I was going through the process I share in this book, without even realizing what was happening.

TO COACHING OTHERS

Sometime later, I discovered the coaching world and built a coaching business (which is an amazing story in and of itself), with a desire to share my own process of shifting from disconnection to connection. Today, I continue to use my life-changing process as one of the world's leading life coaches.

From the start, my entire brand focused on the heart— heart connection, heart-based leadership, heart-centered organizations, and living from the inside out. When I began to coach oil executives, other athletes, and externally successful business owners, I found that my message immediately resonated with them.

Those who had accomplished a great deal in life—who were performers and producers as I had been—were receptive to what I had to say. They were thirsty to create a life connected to their heart, to no longer abandon their heart to produce a result. They finally saw they could have both connection and success.

Today, I continue to inspire and guide people through this process so they can live the connected life. My clients begin what I call "The GREAT Unlearning." It is a beautiful sight to behold. Throughout this book, I will share some of their stories with you.

It's important to note here that many of my stories are related to structures I've encountered along my personal path. I highlight what I've seen in the Christian church, athletics, and business, but you can relate what I share to structures you are more familiar with. The same themes play out no matter the structure because people create them all.

A BEAUTIFUL PROCESS

My goal in this book is to go deep, as I do with my clients. As you dive into you, you will gain a new perspective, and you will be able to apply what you learn to your everyday life.

Along the way, you will discover that what was built out of disconnection falls away, and what was built out of connection remains. In my life, it was humbling to realize how little had been built out of connection. But you only need a seed. You only need one fruit-bearing branch.

In fact, that is all you *ever* had; now you get to let go of the illusion that you have more.

In reading this introduction, you might wonder what you have to lose. You might ask, *What about everything I have accomplished?* And I would ask, *How is that working for you?* We all have two choices—to acknowledge the truth or to remain in the suffering.

You have the opportunity to embody a central truth found in many religions—*to lose is to gain*—but on an experiential level. Yes, letting go is a tender impulse of the heart. And no, you don't need to lose everything. But you do need to be willing to let go of what you want to control. If you aren't, you'll end up losing what you value the most. In the end, the measure to which you let your world sift and sort is the measure to which you will see your life built from love, connection, and freedom.

To navigate through this journey, we will go through three stages—**two downs and then an up**. These stages make up a simple but revolutionary process.

I use this physiological metaphor purposefully. We are going to move from our head, down to our heart and belly, and then up through our creative regions. Here, I'll briefly outline what you can expect in each stage, which correlates to each part of the book.

FIRST DOWN

During the first down, it's time to break through mental constructs. YOU are not your programming...or your parent's, pastor's, or politician's programming. We all live out our zero-to-eight programming if it's not changed, but that doesn't mean the programming is you. You are so much more.

You have held onto certain ways of thinking that once kept you protected but now are hurting you. You can free yourself; you can recognize that beliefs are simply habitual thoughts. In this first stage, you will question your programming—familial, geographical, and religious programming. You will go through a process of unlearning, peeling back the layers of your own BS (belief systems).

By breaking through your mental constructs, you'll see the ways your programming has left you disconnected. You'll see patterns that have remained in your family through generations. You'll let go of residual thinking.

As you go through part one of the book, remember this: just because something is familiar doesn't mean it's right or best for you. We often get stuck in our beliefs. At some point, we might even feel more comfortable with our old programming because it's our normal. When you mess with that hard wiring, it will feel wrong. It *will* feel irresponsible and offensive. And if it does, you're on the right track. Keep going.

SECOND DOWN

Now it's time to move down into the emotional pain— everything you have shut off for years. You're now moving from the head, down into the heart.

First, you will meet anger. At the top layer of this zone is surface frustration and anger. When many people experience anger, their depression also begins to surface because anger turned inward manifests as depression. Anger is at the top, but what is underneath is a lot of sadness and disappointment. Finally, you will move into the lower belly regions, where you feel and connect to the guilt and shame, aka "the wrongness." You must go through all these layers before you can move up.

At this point, you might be thinking, *Brandon this sounds awful. Why the hell would I want to do this?*

Here's why: you can't selectively open. If you are going to open yourself to passion, joy, and peace, you must be willing to open yourself to the pain as well. If you want to go beyond a programmed, numbed-out version of yourself, you'll need to feel it all.

As you move lower, you will sit in a space where you don't have to perform. You can experience your anger, your sadness, and your true emotional age. You might even feel awkward because you can no longer use your gift to cover up your heart. Have you ever used your gifts, talents, and charisma to cover up what's really going on? I know I have.

As you move through your deepest pain, you will be unable to manipulate the world in ways you once could. At this point you will wonder, *What have I done?* You can't even bail yourself out with your performance. But once you hit this place, you're golden.

The only way out is through.

Now, you can build your world FROM a foundation of connection, no longer from a place of pain denial. As you move through this part of the book, remember that pain is not the problem. When we deny our pain, we only add suffering to ourselves and others. When we see pain for what it is, we allow it to flow.

From this place, you will no longer perpetuate the cycle of suffering. You will feel. You will heal. Throughout this process, what you resist will only persist, and what you accept can be transformed.

UP

Now it's time to fire through the creative regions. It's time to penetrate the world from your joy and pleasure centers. It's time to drive forward with power.

At this stage, you feel tuned in, tapped in, and turned on, and you're not sure what to do. It's time to learn how to handle true inspiration and passion. It's time to experience a whole new way of living.

You now have an understanding: you're not here just to survive; you're here to thrive. You're not going to live in the Matrix anymore. You're done with going to work to pay the bills, coming home for dinner, going to kids' games, only to wake up at seventy, disappointed. You're truly out of the hamster wheel and are no longer controlled by the world's expectations. You're not playing that game anymore.

We are in the most abundant time in the history of this planet, and you can take full advantage of that reality now. As you emerge on the other side of this journey, you will know what thriving truly means.

EMERGING

If you are willing to be a heart pioneer, you will emerge as a true leader on this planet.

You first get back your self-respect. That's a win right there. You'll be able to say, "I trust me." Take it from someone who didn't trust himself for so long: I know just how good self-respect feels.

You will also emerge as a true teacher—from a place of congruence. You are not the sage who uses fancy words to get people to look at you. You are your true emotional age, and your words and actions have meaning and power.

In the end, you will be glad you've gone deep because you'll be truly set apart—a city on the hill. The world will recognize the journey you've been on and come to you.

Your desires will come to you, too; you'll be a magnet for what you want.

THE REWARD

Before moving into this process together, I want to make sure you fully understand the reward waiting for you on the other side.

This process does require bravery. In many ways, it will be jolting. But on the other side, you will live by the law of least effort; the least will produce the most. You will see exponential returns, quantum results, grace partnerships.

You will tap into the field of the heart, which is a thousand times greater—electromagnetically speaking—than the field of the mind.

This is not airy-fairy, new age propaganda. What I'm sharing with you is taken directly from my own experience and from science. I have been a firsthand witness to transformation and quantum exponential results. Today, my clients complete the fifteen-year journey I went through in a year.

This process is all about making things real, visceral, tangible, experiential. You have to *feel the lack* so that you can also *feel the abundance* within yourself.

Now, I offer you a gift of grace in the form of this book. You might not like everything I say, but don't shut me off because something I say triggers your programming. Open yourself to the power of this book.

YOU have the opportunity to transform your life and the lives of many others who come in contact with your world.

PHASE ONE

———

DOWN

CHAPTER 1

Pain is NOT Your Enemy

I'll never forget. I was a nine-year-old playing with twelve-year-olds in Little League. The opening ceremony had just wrapped up, and I was the lead-off batter for the first game of the season.

To me, there was nothing bigger in a boy's life. You could smell the hot dogs and feel the excitement in the air.

I felt a wave of energy and determination going up to bat, as I looked at the big lefty on the mound. He had clearly already hit puberty, unlike me. This was man against boy.

I looked over to the third base coach and saw that he gave

me the take sign to not swing. But guess what? On the first pitch, I swung.

The ball went straight up.

From slow motion, life came back into full speed, and my excitement came to a crashing halt. The catcher caught the ball, and I was out. I slammed my bat on the ground, letting out the energy that was still in me and had to go somewhere.

As I walked back to the dugout, I couldn't hold back the tears. My dad was the first base coach, and I knew he was looking. I glanced over his way hesitantly. Even at a young age, I could feel his disapproval of my performance and his embarrassment of how I reacted to my feelings.

All I heard was, "Dry it up, Branny, and get your ass in the dugout," which is West Texan for, "Brandon, stop crying and just hit home runs."

In that moment on the base path, all I wanted was for my dad—the tough, professional bull rider—to see me. What would've happened if he had come down the base-line, grabbed me, and given me a hug, if he'd allowed me to process my emotions and not be scared of how I felt? In that moment, I simply needed his kindness. I wasn't asking for a blue ribbon; I just needed connection in that place of sadness.

As an adult looking back, I realize that was the moment in my life when I started to hide my emotional pain. I (unconsciously) made the decision that how I felt was wrong. My anger was wrong. And my sadness was definitely off limits.

This was when it all started—the moment I disconnected from myself and decided I needed to perform for protection.

The way I saw it, I was left with one option: to abandon how I felt and seek approval outside of myself. In short, I needed to hit home runs. Grand slams, actually. And that was what I did. I hit gram slams all the way to the top.

I progressed as an elite athlete, and by the age of sixteen I was on the US National Tennis Team. I had become a five-time junior national champion, and I played and won a round in the main draw of the US Open. In some ways, this was an amazing journey. But in it all, I shut my heart off, and the by-product was a lack of deep connection with myself and the people around me.

I seemingly had everything: the acknowledgment, the loving family, the people around me. And yet I still felt an excruciating sense of *aloneness*, especially when I wasn't performing.

DENYING THE PAIN

Many family structures are built around pain denial. Out of pain denial, we form mental constructs or coping mechanisms, so we don't have to feel emotional pain. This is called mental protectionism.

We are trained to disconnect within our family, so it's no wonder Thanksgiving is so hard. Everyone is doing their thing, keeping the peace, putting that energy towards making sure everybody's okay. Then they talk about each other to their spouse in the car on their way home.

My parents didn't know how to deal with their own painful emotions and therefore didn't know how to deal with mine. As a result, it took many years for me to really be in touch with what was happening inside of me.

If you grew up in a home with parents who were supportive, especially financially, that doesn't necessarily mean you never dealt with unresolved emotional pain. In fact, you may have felt even more like you had no right to go there.

Take my story, for instance. In many ways, I had an amazing upbringing. My dad owned a company, and he and my mom supported my dreams. They followed good religious principles to stabilize their dysfunction and create a stable energy for us as kids. They were two parents who loved their kids and did the best they could. You couldn't ask for a better childhood.

But at the end of the day, *I still felt alone*. When I hear people defend their parents, I know they're hiding something. If they have to defend their families, they're defending the external persona and denying how they really feel.

IMPENETRABLE OPTIMISM

You probably know people who maintain a certain false optimism in themselves. You find this especially among those who grew up as hyper-achievers.

My family had a high level of what author Gary Zukav calls, "impenetrable optimism." Talking about emotional pain was off limits. It didn't fit their roles. To be good parents, good leaders, a good mom and dad, they felt they couldn't go there. In reality, they just didn't want—or know how—to deal with their own emotional trauma.

Impenetrable optimism is all over the place. It's especially prevalent within spiritual communities. "God is good, brother." "I'm too blessed to be stressed." These are all mentally programmed spiritual statements that are not connected to how people actually feel. It's all spiritual bypassing.

Entire structures are built around mental agreement, doctrinal agreement, religious agreement, or government policy rather than through who people truly are. Impenetrable optimism is found in every space because it comes from the people. It's a way people feel approved of externally. It's a way to keep the peace. It's even a way to hold power. But it keeps us disconnected from ourselves and others.

DISCONNECTION TO IRRELEVANCE

Ultimately, disconnection leads to irrelevance.

At times, I was able to use athletics to feel—to celebrate or to be incredibly angry. But I also used athletic achievement to cover my feelings. After my athletic career (an outlet and an escape), what could I do? There's a reason many men use sports to feel and work to escape. They're not sure what to do with how they feel.

When I left the sports world, I covered up how I felt by being principally good. A lot of people do this, too. And it shouldn't be a surprise that we have a world full of disconnected, principally good people.

But the principles still couldn't cover up what was happening inside of me. I married a smoking hot wife, thinking this would fix me, but things only got worse. I was still looking at porn. I had issues with overeating. I went from 185 to 220. I didn't realize that I needed to go through a process to get back to amazing shape or to no longer need pornography to feel connected or powerful.

Most people don't stop to think about the result of disconnection. For a long time, I didn't either. But what happens when you're numb? You become a shell of who you are and create patterns to disconnect from who you love the most.

Then, before you know it, others see that shell as the new norm. They say, "Well, that's just Dad. That's just how he is. He's just doing what he needs to do to provide for his family."

Really? Isn't there a cost to Dad being so disconnected on a personal level? The answer is *yes*; there's an enormous cost.

When you're disconnected from your heart, the by-product is irrelevance. You become irrelevant to your family and the people around you. You start repeating the same conversations, the same memories, the same stories.

This is why it's rare to see an older person who's relevant. When they perpetuate that cycle of disconnection, they can only tell the "old stories." They slow their speech.

They get hung up on dates and times. I call it the slow fade of irrelevance. It begins the moment you shut off how you feel and align who you are to a role. When it all began for me, I quickly started to think, *I am Brandon, the athlete.*

What role have you taken on?

Maybe you have taken on the role of Provider, Doer, or Super-Mom. No matter the case, you are trading a role for emotional connection, and you are slowly sliding toward irrelevance.

For me, the slow fade of irrelevance started at that moment at the ball game at nine years old. And it didn't stop until I consciously made a shift.

Until I made the shift, I was an expert at romanticizing my experiences and controlling people with my gifts— all forms of mental protectionism, all simply adding to my irrelevance.

PAIN NEEDS A RESOLUTION

I sometimes use the terms "innerG" and "E-motions" to normalize emotions. They are powerful, but they are *inside all of us.* You can think of emotions as *energy in motion* in your body. Like any other energy, emotions need to go somewhere.

When we disconnect from ourselves, all we're doing is putting off the emotional pain and not working through it. This kind of unresolved emotional pain is like a massive balance on a credit card with a high interest rate. Because you're only paying the minimum payment, the balance keeps getting bigger.

If you keep putting it off, you will eventually have to deal with a massive external manifestation of pain. Maybe your business fails, or you go through a divorce. Because you've been unwilling or unable to create resolution around your pain, your world crumbles. This happens so that you can resolve the emotional pain that is within.

In *The Body Keeps the Score*, Bessel van der Kolk explains how our bodies actually store the effects of the trauma and pain we experience throughout our lives. Scientifically speaking, our pain is literally stored away until we deal with it. Our outside world manifests from our internal reality. Breakdowns are unresolved pain that we've delayed recognizing and dealing with.

THE GREAT CONFRONTATION

People ask why I question religion. Why am I disrupting the system, the families? Why am I saying what I'm saying? I question and I speak out because I'm unwilling to ignore.

It's tempting to ignore what is actually happening. It's tempting to simply align to agreements while moving deeper into secret medicating patterns. So many people hold so much that is unresolved in themselves that they have to up their medicating mechanisms. It's a nasty cycle.

In reality, the medicating reveals the root. It's a signpost to something you're avoiding. So what is your form of medication? What are you not willing to confront?

To get to resolution, you must be willing to first feel unstable. When you start to question the stability that has always been there, you're on the right track.

You're allowing the pain to emerge. It's not anything new; the pain existed all along. Now it's simply emerging without protection, without management. With high achievers I work with, they often feel like issues in their businesses are coming out of nowhere as they begin to let the pain emerge. In your life, the suppressed pain is going to come out somewhere as well. Perhaps you're on your second or third marriage, have to file bankruptcy, have kids who don't talk to you, or feel numbed out. What's underneath it all is a big pile of pain. And we have to go there.

This is the **great confrontation**, where everything feels unstable and insecure.

AN ENDLESS SEARCH TO BE SEEN

When pain denial persists without recognition, a person will inevitably search for any possible way to be seen.

One of my clients was raised by two blind parents. Because of his parents' disability, he felt like there were zero places for him to feel or express his emotional pain. He had to take on a leader role from an early age.

He was an expert at playing his role for the family. He became a caretaker. Even though he had several traumatic events happen to him, he wasn't allowed space to process them. His family was simply trying to survive, and he was left out.

One day, he told me a story of coming home from a football game after he threw the winning touchdown. His parents weren't home, so he woke them up early the next morning to share his excitement with them. When his dad rolled over and ignored him, he felt deeply hurt. Not only could his parents not see him physically, but they also couldn't connect emotionally.

His desire to be recognized carried into his life in many ways. Achievement became his medication. He eventually became a CEO, but he felt miserable inside. He had achieved everything from the outside perspective, but he still felt unseen.

Many people try to make achievement their medication, when it's actually a result of their dysfunction. At some point, their achievement actually breaks them down. What got them to the dance, so to speak, isn't keeping them at the dance; it's making them irrelevant, and they don't know what to do with that.

Hyper-achieving can act as a cheap medication for a time, but it won't fill the desire to be seen. For that deep desire to be fulfilled, you must begin to move through this process.

And you must start right here, by first acknowledging the reality of pain—pain that is stored in you from years and years ago, pain that has never been resolved.

What is that pain for you?

A CHOICE

In many ways, you can't help what happens *to* you, but you can help what happens *through* you. You don't have to be a by-product of stimulus and response. Between stimulus and response, there's a choice.

The awareness you're receiving as you read this book will create a wider gap between stimulus and response, so that you can make a different choice.

You don't have to perpetuate the cycle. You don't have to bypass your heart and hit home runs anymore. You can feel what you actually need to feel. You can feel the pain for what it is.

Start there.

CHAPTER 2

You Are NOT Your Reputation

In the Western world, external appearance has become, or perhaps has always been, more important than how we feel internally.

We all try to emotionally protect ourselves through three avenues:

1. **Our reputation**
2. **Our physical performance**
3. **Our material objects**

But you are not your reputation, your physical performance, or your material objects. None of those define YOU. The late great Wayne Dyer was a master at communicating this reality.

The big one here is reputation—how other people perceive you. Without realizing, we live by this belief: *If I can control how I look to the outside world, I can control how I feel.*

In my family, religious servitude fortified our reputation. We did a lot of "good things." We protected the way others perceived us, which in turn protected us.

I believed this lie in my own life and became a prostitute of sorts—a person who's always performing, always dancing, always doing for just a little bit of affirmation.

CONFRONTATION

As we continue moving down in this first phase of the process, you need to ask yourself one important question: *Would I rather look good or feel good?*

I know when one of my clients has decided to switch and actually start feeling good because they start to confront their whole world.

Realigning your life to feeling good is extremely confrontational. It questions all of your beliefs and all of the programming you've picked up along the way. The goal of feeling good might sound airy-fairy, but it actually causes you to address things as they truly are.

Does going to church feel good? If the answer is no, then why are you going to church? Does going to your family's place for the holidays feel good? No? Then why can't you stay home?

The questions you ask yourself might sound a little crazy at first. You might think, *I can't possibly do that.* But what if you took a step back and realized why you are doing what you're doing? What is the reputation that you are trying to maintain? Are you valuing looking good over feeling good?

Here, it's critical to note that you transfer to others how you feel, not what you say you believe. So if you feel obligation, you will transfer pressure onto the ones you love the most. If you truly feel good, on the other hand, you will transfer lightness and well-being to your family, business, and friendships.

If you live your life by this origination point of feeling good, what will happen? I'll tell you what will happen. You'll create a life that feels really good.

But are you ready for confrontation?

THE FEAR OF DISCONNECTION

At the heart of "I am my reputation" is a feeling of aloneness and separation. We fear disconnection, so what do we do? We manipulate others to get them to like us. We won't fully be ourselves because we're afraid of others disconnecting from us.

We learn as children to be the best version of what others want. We say, in essence, "I'm disconnecting from myself to appease you. You can't handle all of me emotionally, so I will shut me off to appease you so that you will approve of me." We do this so we can get some backhanded affirmation. We hope to at least hear, "Isn't she a good girl?" or "Isn't he a nice guy?"

Some people never get to a point where their disconnection builds up so much that they are forced to do something about it. They stay there, in that separation. It's how they survive.

And survival is key in so many circles. When I talk in feel-good language, people get violent, especially in church. Their beliefs have protected them from their past traumas. Now, that cage is being rattled by this new way of thinking, and their emotional violence manifests itself. All of the unresolved hurt and trauma is triggered by a statement like, "You deserve to feel good."

It's interesting to see what comes up with that statement. When people hear it, they either have to shift their paradigm or counter-attack. Ironically, Christians follow someone who did not define himself by his reputation. The Pharisees came after Jesus' reputation, and Jesus told them they had it all wrong. They cared about cleaning the outside of the cup to make it look good. Jesus cared about the heart.

His message was clear: You're not what other people think. You're not what you do. You're not what you have. In short: life is not about surviving by keeping your reputation intact. It's about so much more.

When we live for survival, there's a cost.

In my case, protecting myself through my reputation came with a physical price. My body literally started to break down with all the performing I was doing. After years of over-practicing out of fear, I now sometimes experience difficulty walking at age thirty-nine.

THE TRANSFER WE RECEIVE

When our parents live out of a place of protection instead of connection, we receive a transfer of anxiety and fear.

What I heard from my dad was, "Be the best. Hit home runs every time." What I had heard from my mom was,

"Be perfect. Make great choices. Do the right thing. Be Christlike."

What they were really saying was that they were scared. They were afraid of feeling embarrassed. They were afraid I would make the wrong choice and that my choices would make them look bad and impact their reputation; if I made poor choices, it meant they were poor parents.

You can say a lot of different things, but what you transfer to your children is how you feel. My parents' feelings were saying, "I'm scared. Conform so you don't have to be alone. Separate from yourself. You being you is a little much." And that is exactly what I picked up. The choices I then made kept me from feeling the feelings I needed to feel.

What would have happened if my parents could have opened up about what they feared? There would have been connection for them and for me, and we wouldn't have needed to try to live by a set of principles to keep us safe.

But when the underlying transfer you receive is anxiety, you can't ever just lie down. I remember I couldn't ever just lie on the couch. If my dad walked in, I had to get up.

Why would I have to get up if my dad walked in the room?

Because of an underlying tension that was constantly present. I had to be doing something to be seen a certain way. Feeling tired or resting did not fit in the framework of how I protected myself through performance. And it brought up difficult feelings inside of my parents. My dad, in particular, found it easier to get us moving than to feel his own feelings.

EXTREME LIVING REQUIRES BRAVERY

The way out is an extreme way of living—moving from looking good to feeling good.

In fact, I believe there is nothing greater we can do for ourselves, our families, and the world than to feel good. I'm not talking about the "blessed, not stressed" nonsense. I'm talking about truly feeling good at the core.

If you still aren't quite sure about what I'm saying, I challenge you to start paying attention in your everyday life.

When I come home from work and I feel good, what happens to my home? Do my kids and my wife light up? They do. When Daddy's feeling good, the whole home feels good.

When I'm worried about my reputation, performance, and what I have, how do they respond? Everyone goes their separate ways. They stay away from Dad. In other words, my fear of disconnection has ultimately led to separation.

How much time do we waste worrying about reputation and performance instead of being truly present in the moment? We can't be present with our kids. We miss out on the fun of life. All in the name of protection.

WHAT GOT YOU TO THE TOP

At some point along the way, looking good may have gotten you to where you are. You wouldn't have chosen that path if it didn't have some payoff. But what happens when the business plateaus, and you have to pay the piper? What happens when all the relationships fail, and you have to be real with your emotions? At some point, you will see that what got you to the top will not keep you there.

I work with many leaders who experience this reality. They've climbed the ladder to the top, and now they wonder why they're alone. In a frantic effort to maintain their position, they have to control others more—to be more heavy-handed and rules-based. They end up transferring how bad they feel to everyone else around them.

In order for these leaders to truly elevate in their lives, they have to choose the path of feeling.

AN UPGRADE IN CONSCIOUSNESS

We can also observe the problem with the reputation route from a generational perspective. Let's take fifty-five to seventy-five-year-olds. Many of them have only taken one path, which is head down, performing, working hard, even if it feels bad. Do whatever it takes. Grind it out.

What did they accumulate? They accumulated money along with lots of disconnection. Those around them only wanted what they could get on a physical level.

In the younger generation, we see an upgrade in consciousness. One year at the Grammys, Kanye said, "We got to listen to the kids, bro." It was a mean hook, but it's so true. Listen to what the kids are saying. They're saying there's an easier and better way, a more connected way. They are screaming that message.

My generation is stuck in the middle. We've struggled to accumulate because we've tried to implement two different methodologies—a little bit of the older generation's and a little of this new generation's emotional path. We can't fully trust emotional connection, but we want it, so we take a little from each. For us, it's two steps forward, two steps back.

For this process to work, you must go all the way with feeling good, and that will create momentum. I tell people in my age group—thirty to fifty—that they've got to commit to this path fully. They've got to be radical about it. You have to go after feeling good as a lifestyle.

We live in an age where we can make a lot of money in a moment. We don't have to grind in the fields anymore. We're in the age of computers where we can quantify and calculate information. The speed in which we can do things is so much more exponential, and that's what this new generation is tapping into.

These exponential kinds of results are being proven right now through quantum physics and through heart research. People are studying the electromagnetic frequency of the heart. If you're interested in learning more, go to heartmath.com. There, you'll find research that reveals the power of the heart compared to the power of the brain.

REMEMBER, THERE'S A COST

One of my clients nearly sunk all of his businesses because he was afraid to let go of one business. This is called sunk-cost bias, and it happens when someone has sunk so much money into something that they stop thinking straight.

Sunk-cost bias is caused by someone who holds to

reputation-based value. They keep sinking money into something because they don't want to look bad. My client's big issue was he didn't want to look like a bad businessman and a failure.

If he would've chosen feeling good, he would've lost $250,000 of his own personal money. Instead, he ended up losing over 2 million dollars of his own money. A big difference.

I had to have the courage to dunk his head under the water, sober him up, and say, "This is what you've created, and this is the result." He had to feel some of the pain. Then we needed to address the false programming he had and move toward feeling good at all costs.

The most tender impulse of the heart is *surrender*. Surrender is the entry point into a new, better lifestyle.

Can you surrender? Can you let go of the things you want to hold onto the tightest? My client balked on feeling good and stayed aligned to the old model. There was a major cost for him when he couldn't let go.

SOBER UP

Let's look at reality: most people in the Western world don't feel very good. Most people feel a lot of anxiety, worry, pressure, and false responsibility, even though we live in a time of more abundance than the world has ever seen.

It's no wonder that when we come across someone who clearly feels great and isn't faking it, we feel like we've found a rare jewel.

In order to move past our insistence on survival, we have to keep moving through the process. At this point, we have to be willing to sober up, as my client eventually did.

If you commit to feeling good, you have to feel all the contradiction you've been living in. You have to feel the personal abandonment. You have to feel the aloneness. And you have to recognize that your giving has not actually been giving.

CHAPTER 3

Your Giving Is NOT Really Giving

What would you think if I told you that the good, seemingly noble and generous thing you're doing is actually making you feel disconnected? I want to bust your bubble around giving. What if your giving was a covert way of taking? When we are not willing to take responsibility for how we feel, we end up taking responsibility for others beyond our capacity by over-giving.

Take kids, for example. Why are kids ungrateful when you give them all those things? If true giving returns true gratitude, where's the disconnect? Kids know a gift and they know a take. They know if you're taking from them. Remember, we transfer how we feel, not what we say or do. So if you are giving so that you don't feel scared, they feel the disconnect in the giving. Your gift is covered in a big pile of "I'm scared" energy. Of course, they are going to feel a lack of gratitude.

When it comes to *true giving*, giving within capacity is more connective than giving beyond capacity.

When I was a kid, I was given a lot. I had a lot of opportunity and support, but where was that support rooted? Some of it was rooted out of my dad's own disappointment that he wasn't as good as he could've been as a professional athlete. It was rooted in his inability to follow his own dreams, so he coached us.

I always loved to be on stage; I still love that energy. It was always about the energy for me. In tennis, you keep score for yourself, but I'd always lose track of the score. It wasn't about the score for me. It was about the thrill of coming back and hitting crazy shots.

But that pissed off my dad and my coaches. I remember him asking me one day, "Do you want to work at Taco Bell when you grow up?" It was an underhanded threat to perform and produce that wasn't actually about me. He didn't see why I was in the sport; he could only see through his lens, and all his "support" was tainted with his own pain and disappointment.

FALSE FORMS OF GIVING

This kind of false giving shows up in many different arenas. It certainly shows up in the business world. One of my clients thought he was generous with his employees. After all, a lot of people depended on his company for jobs.

When I dug a little deeper, I found that his giving was actually about him not feeling okay. He needed to be acknowledged as a giver. His role of giver / good leader was a protection mechanism. His giving, which was actually taking, was coming from a place of not ever wanting to feel alone. But even though he gave and gave, guess what he still felt? ALONE.

A lot of volunteers or assistants also love to talk about how much they're doing for others. But do these people actually have anything to give? What is the giving rooted in?

In the Bible, we see Jesus spending time with two women, Martha and Mary. He asks Martha why she is so busy working, while Mary is choosing connection. So many people are just like Martha. They constantly try to gain approval by giving in ways people haven't asked them to give.

If you're running around doing all kinds of things for other people, you're likely writing emotional hot checks.

Making sandwiches Jesus never ordered. Constantly in debt but continuing to believe you're doing the right thing.

Do you continue to give even when your emotional bank account is on empty? Don't be a Martha.

Those who achieve external success in life also struggle with false forms of giving. I experienced this tension when I became a senior pastor at a very early age. The college group I ran became so large that it took away from everyone else's college ministry. I couldn't handle people questioning me; I didn't know if what I was doing was good or not. So I made the table round. I "gave" others positions of authority and crafted a false form of inclusion. In the end, this tainted the very thing that I once loved.

Have you ever tainted the very things that you love because you over-gave? Have you ever experienced not being able to handle the emotional tension inside of yourself and giving away your bread? I have.

OVER-GIVING

You know you're an over-giver when you find yourself resenting others. Somewhere along the way, you started taking false responsibility for everything and everyone. You became an over-giver.

Over-giving leads to resentment, which leads to demonization, and ultimately divorce.

People are over-givers because giving does look good. It's a way to maintain a reputation, and therefore a form of protection. My over-giving was always about trying to make me look better. I couldn't handle the emotions I felt, so I gave beyond my capacity.

Being the responsible one—what's that really about? It's about your fear of being alone and not being able to handle those feelings. You protect yourself by using your gifts. You keep people close by taking responsibility for them. And you can always find people to take responsibility for. After all, very few people want to take responsibility for themselves.

Think about so many family dynamics. The mom thinks, *I'll over-give to my kids so they'll never leave me.* What's really happening here is a form of emotional abuse; the mom is asking the kids to respond in a way they're not supposed to respond. At the same time, the husband thinks, *I'll keep playing my provider role so she won't leave me.* Here again, there's a lot of doing with little emotional connection. I call this "getting backwoods Ozarky" on an emotional level.

What is that root that we're avoiding? What is the mom avoiding? The husband avoiding? The CEO avoiding?

They're avoiding that emotional pain—aloneness, rejection, abandonment, guilt, shame, separation.

To avoid those feelings, we do a lot of things we don't really want to do, and we call it good. We call it god-like. We call it giving.

If we strip off all the layers of over-giving, where are we? Well, we're getting closer to truth.

We're getting closer to, "I don't feel very good. I'm pissed. I'm sad. And I cover all of it up through my over giving." That's what we're driving towards.

And we have to go there.

WHO GETS YOUR LOVE?

I've worked with many individuals who have either physically lost their marriage or emotionally lost their marriage. Sometimes, they're onto their second one and the same thing is being repeated. They found the younger, fitter, 2.0 version, but things are still the same.

Eventually, we see together what is really going on: a whole lot of false responsibility. They have over-given, and the world has gotten their best. In turn, the ones they loved the most got their worst.

We use excuses, saying we must provide for our family because we don't want them to live on the streets. We fortify and justify our disconnection with a role. But something much deeper is going on. We don't know how to deal with our feelings, especially the painful ones.

Once we strip everything away, we see that what we've been running from isn't really that big of a deal. We simply need to acknowledge that we're scared and learn how to process that energy.

DEMONIZING

Demonization always reveals false responsibility. We see this happen all the time in politics and in religious settings. There is a codependent exchange that happens—a mutual accommodation of need.

I need to be powerful and lead. That's how I stay protected. You need to follow. That's how you stay protected. We'll give our power to each other. Then we'll end up resenting each other, blaming each other, and feeling disconnected and not a part of the solution.

When we don't process what we feel, we will blame, resent, and demonize others.

It's absurd that we can demonize each other politically

the way we do in the US. Why is that okay? Where does that come from? We gather with some as a tribe, thereby separating from others, when we do not want to feel. We gather through mental agreement. If we all agree, then we can protect each other from ever having to feel these painful emotions.

Our survival mind justifies our demonization. We believe we have the right to demonize people who believe differently than we do. We truly believe it's a matter of survival.

Mental agreement is what keeps people together in a codependent relationship. *You believe what I believe? Great. I believe what you believe. So we can be connected.*

My wife and I can't even agree on where to go for dinner, much less where we go when we die. If we have to agree on every issue to be in connection, there's some massive conformity happening, and some massive powerlessness taking place, too.

We have to be willing to break that mental agreement model. Otherwise, we will constantly feel disconnected. We will constantly be moving toward divorce in every area of life.

TRUE RESPONSIBILITY

To move to an answer, we must understand true responsibility—the ability to respond.

We must recognize where we feel undervalued and underappreciated. Then we must acknowledge why we feel those things. Is the problem really with your employees or spouse? Is it really that they aren't appreciating your giving? Or did you create a cycle in which resentment and demonization can thrive because you do not know how to deal with what's going on inside of YOU?

To take true responsibility, you need to become an owner of your life and partner with yourself throughout your life. Too often, people want others to do that for them. CEOs often want their employees to take ownership, for example, without first owning how they feel. In the process, they remain subservient (victimized). They let others make decisions for them.

Kids easily fall into this trap; they often want to give their power away. They want their mom and dad to make all the decisions. They don't want to take responsibility for themselves. They are trying to protect themselves from emotional pain by letting others tell them what to do. They give up their power in order to stay protected. That's the exchange. They learn this from YOU, the parent, in how you give your power away to your boss, your church, and the government.

But at some point, each person must decide to be an owner of their own life—the captain of their own ship.

When you take false responsibility, your workers never become owners. Your patrons can never become part of the movement. Your kids will always be subservient and need to rely on you.

FROM, NOT FOR

The twin pillars of true emotional maturity are *protection and provision.*

In order to be an owner and partner in life—in order to truly give—we need to move toward living "from, not for."

"From, not for" gives you a point to return to. Each day, you can ask yourself, *Am I living for something? Am I doing this because I want something from another person? Or am I doing this from a place of love and connection?*

Perhaps you are living FOR protection, constantly handing over your power to the outside world and bypassing yourself.

In a religious setting, you might do all kinds of things you don't want to do so you can have a sense of provision. All the while, you are bypassing yourself.

Perhaps you are living FOR love. Consider your regular conversations with family members. When you talk, are you trying to get love from the other person because you're unwilling to love yourself? What would happen if you showed up FROM love, already having everything you needed?

What would happen if you created protection and provision for yourself from the inside out? Your world would shift. You would no longer need your wife to agree with you on everything. You would no longer need your church or your employees to provide for you in the way they have. Your relationship with all of these would change for the better.

You've given beyond your capacity to stay protected. Now you get to take responsibility for you and let others take responsibility for themselves. You get to live in a whole new structure.

When we learn to live *from*, we live connected and full. We live with power and clarity.

This is also when you get to see where you really are, and it's humbling. The reality for me was, I took a lot of responsibility for a lot of people and their direction in life. When I stopped all the false giving and took responsibility for only me, I could recognize how selfish, rather than self-full, I had been.

CHAPTER 4

———

"Self-fullness" Is NOT Selfish

What's in the cup is for you. What overflows from the cup is for everyone else.

This is the simple message of self-fullness. It's the art of filling one's own cup so that it has the chance of overflowing onto those you love.

Your main job is to fill your cup—to give within your capacity. By so doing, you protect connection within yourself and with everyone else.

Busyness may have once been a signpost announcing, "Aren't I doing good? Aren't I performing well?" Now, it's time to recognize what it truly is—another protective mechanism. If you can't be with yourself or don't know where you're going, you remain busy.

And depletion will only build on depletion. Busyness is no longer a badge of honor and can't stay part of your life if you want to continue in this process.

What we're after is FULLness.

SELFLESSNESS AND SELFISHNESS

The self-full person has something to give. They're not going to take away from you.

Selfless people don't have anything to give, so they're going to take from you. It's that simple. Selfless people are not operating out of their overflow.

Selflessness and selfishness are actually on the same planes of consciousness. Think about selflessness. Why would you want less of yourself? When you're an amazing person at the core, why would you want less?

Selfishness is an attempt to be self-full, but it's sourced in fear and scarcity. Selfish people are trying to fill themselves up.

I prefer someone to be selfish rather than selfless. Selfless people often have a long way to go in overcoming a lot of religious BS, a lot of dogma. But selfish people are at least making an attempt to fill themselves up.

I can work with that.

There was a time that I was obsessed with appearing selfless. I took it as a badge of honor. I was helping to build my dad's company and running a college service. We had three kids under the age of five, and I was juggling a lot simultaneously. I was giving, giving, and giving. And, as you might have guessed, I was completely depleted.

WHERE DEPLETION LEADS

Most people who are depleted are trying to fill their cup with things that give an instant surge, like food. Why is America overweight? It's an emotional issue, not a physical one. Overeating is the quickest way to not feel depleted.

When I was selfless and depleted, I was out of shape and felt terrible. My internal reality started to manifest in my physical body. My habits reflected my internal reality as well, and I no longer had motivation to exercise and gained a lot of weight. Once I switched from being selfless to self-full, I immediately noticed a difference physically.

I see this happen all the time when my clients start to fill their cup from the inside out. They begin losing weight instantly. They become better-looking; they look younger and fitter.

We don't have to focus on their physical health; it takes care of itself. When their insides get healthy, their outsides follow.

Weight gain in the belly is a form of protectionism. The belly is where the guilt and shame are—the deep stuff that we don't want to feel. It's right there in that protective layer. When we feel a need to hide our guilt and shame, we send a signal to the body to protect it. The body protects it by adding layers. Hence the obesity epidemic. When you allow those hidden feelings to come out, you no longer need that extra external layer around your belly.

Sometimes you can observe a person, how they move, how they interact with the world, and you can almost know their story. There is a physical manifestation of what's going on at a deeper level.

Why do old people start to hunch over? What are they protecting? When I am emotionally closed, my hands come in, my shoulders come in. The middle of my back rounds out, and I get smaller. I start to tell the same stories.

What would happen if we became a people who didn't

have to protect those energies, but flowed the emotions instead? We'd live a lot longer and we'd be a lot stronger.

What would it be like for you to be self-full—to live from a full tank of love and value and connection? How would it affect every area of your life?

FILL YOUR OWN CUP

I have seen the radical effects of self-fullness play out in so many of my clients.

When one CEO started filling his own cup, he went from out of shape, hardened belly, and looking terrible to one of the fittest people I knew at his age. Within three years of working together, he participated as an athlete at the Fittest Games for ages forty-five and above.

Another client was a serious alcoholic. As we worked together, he began to give to himself what he was giving to his work and his family. He gave himself time, which allowed us to connect on a weekly basis. He gave himself the opportunity to heal. He gave himself what he had been trying to get from everyone else: APPROVAL. Eventually, he didn't have to focus on his alcohol problem. He didn't need it anymore.

That's when his life truly changed. His family started

coming to him NOT just because of what he could do for them financially, but because he felt great. He didn't have to give and give and give to get love and approval; he was starting to give that to himself.

Everybody wants to be around somebody who feels good and who is connected to themselves. As this man started filling up his cup, his kids could feel that their dad had something to truly give to them.

Anyone can use the add-in method I used with this man. I simply added in feeling good. Jesus taught this same principle in his parable about the wheat and the tares. The enemy came and sowed tares among the wheat. Jesus was asked what could be done. His advice was to allow them to grow together because the wheat would choke out the tares. His basic message was that when you add in the good, it chokes out the bad.

START WITH HONESTY

When you're not full, you use your gift to compensate for that incongruence you feel.

Visionaries, for example, often use their vision gift to paint a massive picture. They promise a trip to the moon, when all they can actually give is a helicopter ride over New York City. What they can give is pretty damn cool, but it's not the promise. They overpromise to get people around them because they don't feel they are enough or that what they can give is enough.

What gift are you using to compensate for the incongruence you feel? Why not instead focus on filling your cup so you actually have something to give?

See the new methodology here? **From the outside in to the inside out.** *FROM, not FOR.*

If you are filling yourself up and you're not overflowing yet, then keep filling yourself up. What's important is not so much the cup overflowing, but the truth of where your cup is. Integrity will ultimately allow you to build true connection, rather than resentment.

How honest are you about your cup?

Growth always comes, first and foremost, from this level of honesty. You can't grow until you acknowledge where you are. When you do, you'll find that what you thought would disconnect you from everyone is the thing that everyone's going to rally around.

What you've always wanted starts to happen because you are honest and real. Your openness begins to lead the way! And it allows others to open up, too.

Honesty is also the way to true peace, as we will see in the next chapter.

CHAPTER 5

Keeping the Peace Is NOT the Same as Making Peace

What you've called peace is probably not peace. It's pseudo peace; it's pain denial.

Keeping the peace doesn't get what you want. Rather, it keeps you capped in a space of non-confrontation. You use your great gifts and abilities to navigate (manipulate) emotionally, but it doesn't get you anywhere.

A couple years ago, my daughter broke her arm all the way through. Imagine that we had just put Neosporin on it. She would have never had the use of her right arm for the rest of her life.

That might seem like an obvious conclusion, but we don't think the same way about emotional brokenness. Keeping the peace is, emotionally speaking, like putting Neosporin on a broken arm; it keeps people (yourself included) disabled and limited.

LET'S GET REAL

How does this actually play out? Well, let's consider that scene at Thanksgiving. You've got everybody coming into one house, most of whom are probably trying to keep the peace. As a result, there are a lot of unsaids.

Of course, when everybody goes into their rooms or gets back into their cars, the explosion of true feelings come out. "Can you believe so-and-so?" "The gall of that person." "I'm glad we're out of there because I couldn't handle this anymore."

What really happened? What happened was no more than toleration. Everyone kept the peace until they didn't have to be in each other's presence anymore. Everyone maintained a place of pseudo connection and behavior modification.

It's no wonder so many people loathe going to family events. It's not that we don't have a deep love for family, but keeping the peace is tough to navigate. You can't hide what's really there for long.

For many, going to work is the same as Thanksgiving. Are you going to that place you go every day, knowing that you have to keep the peace? That's draining. It takes massive amounts of energy to just grin and bear it. Maybe you don't grin and bear it and instead release your emotional tension through gossip. But that's not the answer either. How much is the gossip costing you and the company? There has to be a better way.

But what is this peacekeeping really all about? Why will people not be honest about how they feel, and why are they busy doing what they don't want to do? Those are the questions we've got to address.

ALIGNING TO ROLES

Aligning to the role of peacekeeper is actually a protection mechanism.

Keeping the peace at Thanksgiving is actually selfish. All the hosting, cleaning, and biting your tongue looks selfless. But really, we just don't want to feel the internal tension that is triggered if Aunt Susie and Uncle Sam have another spat. So we stay in our ROLE. We don't want to feel the discomfort, so we do everything we can to avoid it.

In our family, my mom played a big role in keeping the

family together. She's a very talented and powerful person, and she put a lot of energy into the role of mom. Her desire to create peace and stability was not all bad or wrong, but it limited her.

My dad, on the other hand, played the provider role, a role that many men align to so that they don't have to connect emotionally. They get a hall pass. Mom tells the kids to make sure Dad's okay because he's been working hard and does great things for the family. Dad aligns to that role so he can stay emotionally distant.

TIME FOR A FAMILY MEETING

About ten years ago, things came to a head in our family, and we actually decided to make peace instead of keep on keeping the peace.

There are four of us kids. My little brother was single, and the rest of us were there with our spouses. We all shared and were open and honest with my parents about how we grew up.

We told our mom we wanted more for her than just being our mother. She is an amazingly gifted and talented person, who put so much energy into being a mom. But we also wanted more for her. Some of our words connected and some didn't.

Even my little brother was a real catalyst in that moment. He and my dad have a little more chill mode. Everyone else is type A to the max. In this moment, he brought up how we couldn't simply chill together as a family. We couldn't simply connect; we had to always be doing something.

What my mom heard was, "Everything I've built my life on, my role as a mom, has not been good." She heard, "I failed. I'm bad. I'm wrong." What started to crumble was that role that had protected her heart for a long time.

My mom is a very charismatic, strong woman, but to see her run into her bathroom and then lock herself in the closet shook all of us. She crumbled before our eyes and hid out for a couple days.

Oftentimes, when you make peace by having courageous conversations and being honest, what people hear is that they are wrong or bad. They feel attacked. But those same walls that people put up to protect themselves are the same walls that keep love out.

After a couple of days of all of us having a vulnerability hangover, my mom emerged. She felt a lot of the feelings she had been avoiding by playing small. She came out of that closet, giving herself permission to move beyond her role as mother and step into her authentic, badass self.

After this point, my mom truly entered into the process I share in this book and literally transformed herself. She is one of my biggest heroes!

A DIFFICULT CONVERSATION

Understand that this is not a one-time deal. In no way am I trying to minimize how difficult these conversations are. When you go here on a personal level with your family and with yourself, you have to be ready for a process. You have to give it time.

Peacemaking can be so much harder with those who are closest to us. This is why coaching is so important. Somebody outside of us can see us and say the same things that the people closest to us in our lives would say. But we can accept it and see it differently from a coach.

People sometimes tell me their parents are seventy or eighty years old and could never handle this process of honesty. What they are saying is that *they* themselves cannot handle it. They are forty or fifty years old and are still scared to be honest with their parents. They have chosen to stay victimized by their parents. It's actually more about you than it is about them. Are you going to shut down, or even tone it down, because people don't do the same, or are you going to continue to play from the inside out no matter what?

We all want to be around people with whom we can be ourselves. But to get there with those you are closest with takes a lot of bravery. Are you still playing scared with your parents? It's time to fully be honest with yourself and the world.

Lastly, I know that some might read this and think that talking to their parents in this way feels dishonoring. I would challenge you to acknowledge that talking *about* your parents behind their back is what is actually dishonoring. The truth is that you don't want to express yourself fully around those you love, and so you call it dishonoring.

Keeping peace is a very low level of integrity. Making peace requires you to be honest with yourself and with others. Making peace is actually the highest form of integrity and congruence.

Remember the broken bone? It hurts to have to re-break that bone. There is pain in resetting that bone. But don't you want to live with a fully capable limb? Don't you want your family to do the same? It's unloving to allow others to walk with a limp when you have tools of honesty that could help them run free.

WHAT WE REALLY WANT

Many of us keep the peace because we don't want

to lose what we have. In the process, we become more disconnected.

I had a young female client who was doing everything in her company, including serving as a CEO. She used her extreme ability to get things accomplished in order to keep the peace everywhere she went. She didn't want to feel the fear of loss, so she micro-managed and second-guessed her team.

Like so many other great leaders do, she had become a manager. The sad part was that she was a ten as a leader. She was called to inspire her team. But she chose to dumb herself down to control her environment and keep the peace.

Can you relate? Are you a leader who is micro-managing out of fear?

My client not only tried to control everything but also turned to alcohol because she felt depleted. Things got so bad that she was only able to have sex with her husband if she was drunk. In turn, she felt a lot of guilt and shame.

Together, we moved to a place where she could identify what she was scared of. Why did she become a peace-keeper/manager in the first place? For her, she was scared she would feel alone and that her business might not succeed if she let go of managing everything.

She stayed up in her head, doing what she knew how to do because she wasn't willing to feel pain and address the deep emotions.

What we all truly want is on the other side of this first down. We have to keep moving into our hearts and the deep energy that hangs out in our lower belly. But we stay up in our heads because we're afraid. We keep the peace, we conform, we settle.

For me, to get my dad's heart, I'd either perform really well or instigate. In either case, I knew I could get some attention from him. A lot of kids use anger and frustration to get attention. At least they're getting closer to their parent's heart. Many wives instigate their husbands to get some kind of response. They're just trying to get to that heart. Then the husband explodes, and she feels she got some form of connection from her instigating. A cycle is formed for connection.

But there's a truer way to connection. And it will require us to go a little deeper—*past even our mental constructs and initial obstacles to feeling our pain.*

We have to move down—into the heart.

PHASE TWO

——

DOWN

CHAPTER 6

There Is No Greater Pain Than Abandoning Your Own Heart

When I was in school, I did a project that required me to interview a family member. I interviewed my granddad's fiancée and asked her about growing up as an orphan. Through our conversation, the realization hit me: I felt like she did growing up.

Since she was actually an orphan, her experience was more exaggerated and amplified. I remember how she described having to do things she didn't want to do for love. In her case, there was sexual abuse involved. I could tell it all felt closer to the surface for her. But when I got to the bottom of it—when I laid my head down on my pillow at night—I felt what she felt.

I felt alone.

In *Experiencing the Father's Embrace*, Jack Frost talks about the orphaned heart. It is not a well-known book, but it provides a great description of the orphaned heart, which is a heart that does not feel protected or provided for.

As I shared, I grew up in a physically amazing home. I had two parents, never worried about a meal, went to church, and generally enjoyed stability. Yet, my heart still felt orphaned. It's strange to say that I felt alone when I grew up in the Western world and was parented by baby boomers who wanted to give their kids everything. But I did.

That's a pretty big conundrum, but it's where we are as a society because we can't connect with the pain. And when you can't connect with the pain, you can't connect with the joy. Brene Brown has taught us that we can't selectively feel. By not acknowledging the separation we feel, we can't align to the courage of our hearts.

THE CYCLE OF DEMONIZATION

There is nothing more painful than leaving a situation

without speaking up for yourself, being real, and being seen for who you are.

So what do we do with that pain after we leave a painful situation? Rather than recognize the pain for what it is, we often gossip about that person we were with or demonize the situation.

In America, this cycle of demonization has become so common that we think it's normal. We don't see that our own pain is emerging because we feel unsafe. We don't know what to do with our feelings of insecurity, so we retreat or attack. Remember, what you resist only persists. All emotional pain wants is one thing: resolution. If not resolved, it will manifest through the collective in some unsavory ways. Demonization of others is a manifestation of unresolved emotional pain in individuals.

I believe that most violence on the planet stems from personal abandonment. When people abandon their hearts, they use their gifts to overpower and control. Whether it's gun violence or "keyboard warriors" attacking others online, violence is the quickest way for the emotionally abandoned person to feel powerful.

Southside Chicago's gun violence is not a gun problem; the problem is emotional abandonment. Abandonment breeds powerlessness, and to regain their power, people wield the gun or the tongue and harm others.

And the cycle of violence repeats.

THE TOP LAYER

At the top of the second 'down,' we find frustration and anger. And later, we find that anger turned inward is depression.

This emotional pain is central to this entire process. Yet, we are taught that this top layer is wrong. But why wouldn't I show anger or sadness? Why do I think it's wrong?

There is a mental construct that keeps us thinking that way. In most family structures, emotional pain is the enemy. So we have built a culture that says emotional pain—anger, sadness, and depression—is wrong. It actually threatens the foundation upon which we have built our institutions.

Many look for value and reputation based on what others think. But others' reactions do not validate the pain; their reactions only reinforce its wrongness. So we go on living protected by our reputation and ignoring the emotional pain altogether.

The problem is that this game doesn't work. Most people

live frustrated, and eventually the anger comes out one way or another. And as soon as it does, many lose confidence in themselves. They immediately go back to protecting themselves. They go back up to their heads—to their principles and mental constructs.

I see this layer much differently. The moment I know I've gotten a client's anger, I know I've gotten their heart, and I'm starting to get more of that emotional layer. I'm diving down. I tell them, "Thank you for the anger and the depression. That's good. Let's keep going."

Why do we adopt limiting beliefs? We do it to protect ourselves and others from our anger. When we start to feel that we can't do something, we go up into our mind and adopt protective beliefs to keep us safe.

Because we are not taught to deal with the feeling of disappointment, we create an emotional foundation of rejection. We reject what we really want and attach to a limiting belief. What happens if you know how to process these feelings? You no longer need the limiting beliefs to keep you safe.

There's a reason people will get more rigid with their religious beliefs when they don't feel they can trust themselves. If they have an affair or go to prison, they will adopt radical religious beliefs, thinking these radical mental principles will protect them. They may go off the rails on alcohol and then go all in on AA, which then becomes their new addiction. Once they feel something is wrong, they drive back up into their head, into the mental conceptualization.

Remember that *mental conceptualization is fortified through agreement.* You agree with a religious doctrine or political party to keep yourself safe. Then you modify your behaviors to fit in. Yet, all the while, there might not be anything real happening at an emotional level. It's all conceptual. And you stay there to avoid the abandonment inside.

What if your zealous relationship with your faith or political party was not about what you are saying it's about? What if it was about emotional provision and protection? In my own life, I started to see that my over-commitment to these was actually a reaction to feelings of abandonment.

When you protect from the outside in, you judge externally what is safe or not safe. You become a judgmental asshole and view people based on their beliefs only, so that you can stay protected.

By going down to this first layer, you have to switch *from the outside protecting you to the inside protecting you.*

Not only will your heart protect you, but it will allow you to live a life *from* protection and provision, not *for* it. When you try to live *for* something, you will never obtain. When you live *from* something, you have already obtained it. Living *from* ensures that you already are that which you seek.

The emotions (anger, sadness, and depression) you feel are not wrong but are actually the energies you need to produce greater clarity, authentic power, new levels of flow and abundance, and ultimately, connection in your life.

WHAT YOU RESIST PERSISTS

Psychologist Carl Jung coined the phrase, *What you resist persists*. I have found this to be consistently true. What is just as true is that *what you accept can be healed and transformed*.

Look, for example, at the Christian church's resistance to talking about sexual sin. Where is the most pornography viewed? It's viewed in the most religious places on the planet because everyone is trying to resist something, which only gives that thing more energy.

In the same way, resisting pain only brings more pain into your life. The root emotion is not wrong; what's wrong is a lack of acknowledging.

When I used to feel a lot of energy inside of me and it started to stimulate me, I didn't know what to do with it. I wasn't taught how to deal with my internal reality, so when things started firing inside of my body, all I knew to do was to get a cheap release.

Masturbation isn't only about getting your rocks off when you feel stimulated. You can masturbate your emotional energy when you get excited or inspired. Think of a time that you listened to something that got you fired up or gave you an amazing business idea. When you went to tell someone, they probably poopoo'd all over the idea. This was you masturbating your emotional energy. What would happen if you knew how to hold it and let it marinate in your body? Instead of telling someone, you let that flow of internal energy lead you down the path of inspired action. Ultimately, people would see the creation of your inspiration, not your words only.

Most people are not trained how to handle their energy in motion, that energy that is firing inside of them! They resist it, medicating with cheap releases. All the while, the root of the anger and sadness persists.

What if you did not run away from the anger and the sadness and were able to be with the emotions until they resolved? You'd be a badass, that's what! Bye, abandonment, and hello, connection.

ARE YOU LEFT OUT?

Many leaders and businesspeople prostitute their gifts for approval. They play the role of organizer and peacekeeper, the one who rallies everyone together, but all the effort comes at a high cost to their heart.

Many salespeople also prostitute their gift of charisma, communication, and action (their catalytic ability) for a small return. They say, "I *need* to make this work somehow. I'm going to do whatever I have to do to make this work." They fear what will happen if they don't make it work. In the process, they miss themselves. Their heart gets put on hold.

When someone is constantly giving, doing, and selling, they might get something in return, but they usually get left out of the big deals. For this salesperson, the big deal is always right around the corner, just out of reach.

Why? Because big deals only happen on a vibration of value.

Don't wig out on me here just because I said the word vibration. Here's what I mean: We are like radio towers. We emit a frequency, and the corresponding vibration returns back to us. Our mind vibrates at a certain frequency, and our heart / internal reality vibrates at another frequency. As mentioned earlier, our heart vibrates, electromagnetically speaking, at a rate 1,000 times greater than our programmed mind.

You can't fake your vibration.

We live in a vibrational world. If you're taking manic action and prostituting your gift with your programmed mind, you're not operating on a vibration of value but a vibration of need, which has a much lower vibration. If you are connecting with how you feel and step into inspired action from connection, you will create results that are 1,000 times greater than you could using your programmed mind.

For some time, I worked with an owner of a large manufacturing company in Texas. From the start, I could see his gift was connecting people, but he prostituted his gift for approval over and over.

He would bring people together, but he would get left out. His wife told him he needed to stand up for himself. But he wasn't sure how to have the courageous conversations that he needed to have to get the deal. It was easier for him to give his gift than to be honest. It was harder for him to say to a friend, "I'm not going to connect you unless I'm a part of this deal." It didn't feel good to say that. It didn't feel like friendship.

Why didn't it feel good to him? When he would stand for

himself, his energy in motion, or emotions, would start to rattle. Since he was not familiar with these emotions he would abort what he wanted. He would say it didn't feel good or didn't feel like friendship. In reality, he simply did not know how to deal with the energy in his body as he was elevating.

In turn, he was stuck in a cycle of gift-based connecting. He was disconnected from his heart and therefore disconnected from the big opportunities. In order to move to a different place in his career, he had to reconnect to his heart. He had to feel the frustration that was actually there.

If you can relate to this business owner's experience, it's time to step back, create white space, and do less. What will less open you up to? That's when you feel what's really going on. If you're not taking manic action and prostituting yourself, what are you left with?

Do you feel anger and sadness? Start there. If you don't, you won't ever be able to get to a vibration of 1,000 times value.

In this process of reconnecting to your heart, you will also re-align to your emotional age. This is when things get exciting.

CHAPTER 7

Aligning to Your Emotional Age

Have you noticed how many people can't remember much about their childhood?

We might remember the pain because pain was the only thing we ever experienced deeply. And at some point, the pain was too much, so we shut ourselves off completely. In the end, all we're left with are mental concepts of family and protection mechanisms.

In order to actually mature emotionally, we have to go backward to where we cut off our emotions. Our physical and emotional age need to come into congruence. We have to close that gap. And when we do, some extraordinary things happen.

FACE WHAT YOU FEEL

The problem, once again, is that it's not easy to face what we truly feel. I've worked with several clients who said their families were awesome, only to later find out they were abused. They shut themselves off with that impenetrable optimism. And because they are great masterminds, they find a way to protect themselves by staying in their heads.

However, the moment one of my clients steps into their true emotional age and communicates from where they really are emotionally, they become the leader wherever they are. It's a powerful thing to witness.

I hold Master Heart events where my clients come together. During one of these events, I had a man attend who was on the board of directors of one of the largest transportation companies in the world. When he allowed himself to feel his true emotional age, the whole room was sucked in, and he became the instant leader. He became relevant.

When you connect to your emotional age, you become relevant.

This man was honest about what was happening inside of himself. He was honest that he felt internally broken, disconnected, alone. He didn't feel good with his wife and wasn't attracted to her anymore. The moment he allowed himself to go there and be real was the moment that a door was opened for everyone else. They all knew he was being real. Only then was his great genius able to emerge.

In a group of high achievers, there's always some posturing that happens. When that one person breaks out and owns their realness, the whole room is sucked in like a vacuum to that energy. You can actually see it happening. Everyone moves forward; that person has everyone's attention.

Guess what happened to the man who connected to his emotional age? His passion has reemerged for his wife because he took the lid off of his heart. His kids see him as relevant. He's enjoying the money he's made and is creating amazing family experiences from it. He's even pursuing his passion of public speaking.

To close this gap with my clients, I often start at age eight to ten, since these are helpful reference points. If you own a corporation and actually feel eight inside, you need to start there. What are the core values of an eight-year-old?

You're a CEO but just want to play like a ten-year-old? Great. What do ten-year-olds do? You ride bikes with your buddies. Since you're a little older, you could go for the Harley.

The goal here is to *get back to a place of congruence*. It's so beautiful to see these top leaders insert fun, passion, and play into their lives and their businesses. It's also amazing to see how their world responds to their newfound FUN!

BUT WON'T THOSE EMOTIONS HURT OTHERS?

One of my best friends came out to California about five years ago to visit. He came to one of my kid's basketball games that I was coaching, and right in the mix of it he said, "What the hell happened to you? You're one of the most cutthroat competitors I've ever met, but you're not acting like yourself."

What he knew was that while my words were saying one thing, my heart wanted my sons to be badasses. I wanted to say, "It's time to dominate. It's time to do this thing." But what I was communicating was, "Let's make sure we pass the ball, guys."

I looked at my friend after he talked to me at halftime, and I looked back at the kids. I said, "Guys, here's what I want. I want y'all to kick their ass." A bunch of eight-year-olds looked at me strangely. I told my son, Connor, "I want you to score as many points as you can and dominate this game. Go be awesome!" He wasn't sure what to think.

But can you guess what ended up happening? They passed

the ball more than they'd ever passed. They were kinder to the players on the opposite team. They experienced a freedom to be themselves because I was being myself. When I wasn't myself, they felt like they had to fight for their greatness.

I remember a time my own dad showed his true emotional age, and it meant so much. As I was going through the deconstruction with my church and bringing this message to the congregation, one of the pastors who had a mega church in my city, who was a mentor of mine at the time, butt-dialed me. I listened to his conversation with another pastor as they talked about me and said some pretty awful things.

When I told my dad and some leaders of our church, I started crying. My dad stood up and said, "I want to beat the shit out of them right now."

He grabbed me with the intensity of a professional bull rider. I've always known that intensity to be there, but he rarely showed it to us because he felt like it was out of control and not right. The only time we got to see that was when we were disciplined.

But this time, I felt my dad's heart. I felt how deeply he was affected by what happened. He wasn't being the perfect spiritual leader; he was simply being real and raw. At that moment, all my own anger and pain dissipated, and I could be my full self and love those two pastors. I could see the situation for what it was.

Of course, there's a difference between projecting your anger onto someone and allowing your anger to be felt and seen. So many people have experienced anger, especially from a coach or a father, and it hasn't been out of that connective place. Instead, it's used against them.

I am not an advocate for projecting your anger—the Bobby Knight type of leadership of projecting anger onto an official or players, which is actually based in fear. I am an advocate for being honest with where you are. I am an advocate for connection.

When you're with your kids, are you being real? When you're with your wife, are you willing to air your frustrations and ask her to hold your hand as you have those feelings? Those emotions don't hurt others. They connect you to others.

HEART VULNERABILITY

There is a difference between mental transparency and heart vulnerability. Mental transparency is the low road, while heart transparency is the high road that leads to real connection and inspired action.

I love seeing employees take the high road with their supervisors. In one case, an employee practiced heart vulnerability by explaining how he felt shut off whenever his supervisor made fun of one of his questions.

The employee literally elevated the conversation beyond criticism and got straight to the heart of the matter. Sadly, the supervisor was unwilling to take this high road of heart vulnerability and instead brought sarcasm into the conversation—criticizing the employee again. Because he couldn't deal with the energies inside of him, he went back to protecting himself.

I challenged the supervisor to move off of the low road of mental transparency—simply saying whatever came to mind about his employee. I asked him to move beyond protection and to share what he actually felt and what he actually wanted. With some guidance, both the employee and supervisor were able to share their hearts. Through an honest conversation, they could then consider what they were willing to do with what they felt. It was a beautiful moment, a moment that unfortunately doesn't happen enough in the business world.

Do you find yourself taking the high road or the low road? What do you do with those turbulent energies in motion inside of you—that aloneness, fear, and pressure? What are the habits you've created as temporary solutions?

Do you criticize others because you're not good with the turbulent feelings within yourself?

That had become a pattern of mine. I would criticize the ones I loved, pointing out any little flaw I could find. That felt easier than dealing with what was happening inside of me.

Most people move toward destructive patterns. Some move toward something a bit better for release. They might be addicted to working out, for example. In either case, they haven't aligned to the feelings they actually need to feel.

Sometimes, when I talk about emotional age, people ask me if I'm telling them to go to a strip club, or to eat all the chocolate cake, or to cheat on their spouses. I respond, "Well, you're already doing it. That stuff is already happening." Your pornography addiction. Your binge eating. All I'm saying is let's get real with it. Let's be honest and upfront. When we are open with what's really going on, the emotional energy can be used for inspired action instead.

What are you looking for in a strip club? The intimacy, the touch, the smell, the closeness? What if you were instead open and honest with others to get the intimacy you were looking for? Even better, what if you knew how to give that to yourself? All of a sudden, you don't need that external solution as a temporary substitute. You don't need the chocolate cake to cover over the deep anger and sadness.

BEING HONEST WITH YOUR LOW ENERGIES

What we've deemed as wrong is actually the thing that feels the most protective and connected. And what is connective leads to what is most loving.

Most depression happens to the deepest feelers. They've shut off that part of them to produce, and now they're paying the piper. They think it's wrong to experience depression, and they feel a resistance to it.

They might begin to make excuses, saying they wouldn't make money or wouldn't have a job. Maybe they're not willing to feel the depression because they don't know where the bottom is. Maybe they had family members who were heavily medicated or committed suicide. Maybe they're afraid that they will be in their bed for three months.

But here's the thing: depression is calling the body to deep rest. It's calling the person away from performance mode for a reason.

What if we were there for our anxiety, our anger, our sadness—all of these low energies? What if we were there for them like we would be for a newborn baby, at that level of tenderness?

If we truly feel those low energies, the energies can actually flow. Every negative emotion just wants resolution. That's all it wants.

That's why the healing process is a physical thing. These trapped emotions inside your body need resolution. Hindus call emotional traumas that want resolution Samskaras. They want release.

But it is painful for these traumas to be released—to unknot and unravel. From a psychology standpoint, part of the brain literally shuts off to forget trauma. When it comes back years later, you have to go through all of those emotions again. What you're not told is that trauma goes somewhere in your body. We might shut it off with our mind, but the trauma—that energy in motion—gets stored in our bodies. It still wants resolution.

When you allow yourself to feel and unknot, some of the memories will reemerge. When you allow the internal energy to be seen and felt, the emotional trauma will no longer have control over your life.

We must have awareness and acceptance for these emotions. When we're tender with them, they will actually inspire us to action. When they flow, they will speak to us. They actually hold amazing information for us. I have seen this be true time and time again.

FROM FANTASY TO FOCUS

So many people are afraid to be afraid. But we all feel afraid. If I'm getting ready for a tennis match or a public speaking engagement, I face a feeling of fear just like you would. But I allow this feeling to be there for what it is. In fact, I've come to allow a safe place even for terror.

When we don't allow these feelings, we're left to fantasize. In fantasy land, we can't actually be rooted and grounded in what we truly desire. Instead, we try to be whatever we feel like we need to be. And that keeps us away from a healthy, focused energy.

When you think you need to be a certain age, you wander and search because you don't actually know what you feel. You become a chameleon, and you even get praised for it. But you know this is costing you deep connection with YOU and others.

When someone becomes their emotional age, they may be a little rowdy and immature for a while, like a teenage kid. They may drop a few more f-bombs than they typically do. But all along, they never wanted perfection; they wanted connection. And out of their newfound connection, they're more focused on what matters most, and thus become FAR more effective leaders. They know what they actually feel, and others know it, too.

They are leaders who are willing to face every emotion for exactly what it actually is—even the emotion many people fear most: sadness.

CHAPTER 8

———

It's Okay to Feel Sad

What is underneath the anger and the depression? It's just a big ball of sadness that life isn't working out or this moment isn't working out.

Allowing yourself to feel sad is not wrong and not something to be avoided. As with all the other emotions, sadness provides a chance for healing.

To this day, I allow myself to write songs of sadness in my journal because it's healing to recognize sadness and process it. Sometimes, I even post these on Facebook, and so many ask, "Are you okay?" I appreciate their good intentions, but I'm more than okay. We should be worried when people aren't willing to show their sadness. It's healing to let it come out in whatever way it wants to come out. We all need this kind of release.

A CONVERSATION WITH MY DAD

A couple years ago, I had a tough conversation with my dad over the phone. I told him I'm a grown man and still scared of him. I was honest and told him that a big part of me was really thankful for him but that another part of me hated him.

The moment I said it, I could feel this ball of energy inside of me release, like I was giving up something that was close to me for a long time.

He was very open to hearing what I had to say and wanted to know more. He didn't shut me down. He had the ability to hear me, which is a testament to how far we've come in our relationship and how far he has journeyed into his heart. He wanted to make sure I said everything.

So I said the hardest thing for me to say. I wanted to know what I was like as a little boy, from his vantage point. The moment I said that, I started bawling and hyperventilating. I was disoriented and couldn't catch my breath because it was such a massive energy release that I wasn't expecting.

When I calmed down a little, he began to tell me who I was as a child and how special and gifted I was, how everyone wanted to be around me. He shared how I had an 'it' factor. In that moment, he really doted on me and affirmed my specialness.

Hearing those words from my father felt really good. I was getting back to who I really was.

I'll never forget the end of the call. He said, "Branny, if there's anything else you want to tell me, I want you to call and tell me." What do you think has happened to our connection since that point? My dad has become highly relevant to me—far beyond physical provisions. Very few parents become more relevant to their children as they age, especially on an emotional level.

At that moment, he wasn't telling me things I should do or say. He just wanted to know more of me and what was happening inside of me. It all started with anger and with allowing myself to hate my dad and express it. Then came the deep sadness underneath, followed by massive connection.

When we cry out all the pressure and resistance, we break through a wall. With this simple conversation, I stopped a pattern in my family. I could have guaranteed that my kids would hate me by not going there with my own dad because *energy that's not resolved is transferred and re-created.*

At the time of writing this book, my kids are thirteen, twelve, and nine. They know they can tell me about any pain they feel towards me and that we can talk about it. That connection is already there.

BE WILLING TO EXPERIENCE THE OPPOSITE

Some people lie because they're emotionally disconnected, but emotional dishonesty is lying, too. When
we're willing to be honest about our sadness, we're also
able to move toward congruence and connection in every
area of our lives.

This is true in the business arena as well. One client never
felt he could express all his anger. When he finally did,
what ended up revealing itself was all the sadness and
hurt underneath. For the rest of the day, I sat with him as
he went through deep crying sessions. By the end of the
day, his connection to sadness allowed him to connect
to what was real.

Connecting to what was real in his business gave him the
ability to see what he couldn't before and make decisions
that resulted in massive financial returns for himself and
the people that worked for him. Connecting to the pain
and feelings (the soft topics) produces hard results. In this
case, connecting to the pain of his emotions gave him the
ability to transform his company!

Emotional dishonesty costs businesses large amounts of
money each year. Think about where you work. Are you
emotionally honest with your team? How much doesn't
get accomplished because you cannot be honest with
what you want? Why can't you be honest? Because when

you state what you want, feelings surface, and feelings want to be resolved. It seems easier to go around people and issues than it does to address what is really going on inside of you.

Here are three questions you can ask today:

1. **What am I feeling?**
2. **What do I want?**
3. **What am I willing to do about it?**

Answer these, and you will step into a level of emotional honesty that brings safety and trust to your world.

Again, you can't see the good in a connected form if you're not willing to experience the opposite. If you want your kids to have true gratitude for you and their world, you will allow them to feel the negative emotions, too. If they aren't allowed to do this, they will not be able to contact the gratitude as well.

Deep laughter can be very healing, as well as yawning. I notice that when people start to yawn, they're allowing themselves to feel the tiredness of performing.

As you move into deep sadness, let the messiness of the process be whatever it is. The messiness is so beautiful, so connective, so real, and liberating. There might be laughter. There might be yawning, as you release the exhaustion of performance. Your body may want to shake like a dog shakes off after almost getting hit by a car.

Whatever comes, let it. It's the doorway to freedom and connection.

CHAPTER 9

Easy Doesn't Mean Sleazy

At this point in the process, you are tired of the mental finagling, the manipulation of yourself and others, the bypass.

You realize there is no greater pain than the pain of abandoning your heart. The totality of you is sad—sad because you've bypassed your heart and bought into manic action or production. You've believed that doing enough would make you feel like enough.

Now is where the letting go happens. Now, we step into a deep rest. We create white space in our lives for what comes next. You can't connect to what is happening inside of you if you are busy doing. During this season of the process, the external fluff (people, habits, even opportunities) starts to fall away. Don't worry—you'll see that is a good thing.

POST-MANIPULATING, CONTROLLING, AND DENYING

Depending on your personality, you have either manipulated yourself or tried to control your world so that you don't have to feel. Either way, you have denied what's really going on.

If you're an external visionary, an energetic action taker, you tend to manipulate yourself and others to produce, so you don't have to feel. You make statements like, "Just trust me." The end always justifies the means with this crew. There's a lot of external promising of future outcomes. I am personally a manipulator when I'm not willing to feel my feelings.

The controllers are very task-oriented people and high achievers, so they achieve a little more through detail. They are motive-based and ask why a lot. They don't have to control the whole world. They just try to control the most powerful person, and that's all they need. They let the most powerful person manipulate everyone else. They're used to feeling victimized by that person they're trying to control.

The deniers are our peacekeepers. They are very loyal, sharing individuals and possess peace and stability. If they deny something long enough, then it's not true. They live a lot of their life asleep to what's really going on.

In my coaching work, the trait that makes me different than others is that I don't get hung up on my clients' behavior, and I'm usually the first person in their life not to.

If manipulation, control, or denial have shown up in their life, I don't get hung up on it. I know that when the heart is transformed, behaviors take care of themselves. At this point in the process, no matter what personality you have, it's time to let go of manipulating, controlling, or denying. It's time to just be with what is.

"COME TO ME ALL WHO ARE WEARY AND HEAVY LADEN"

The great ancient teachers talked about the yoke of performance being heavy. True salvation, whatever it means to you, is embodying a truth that says you don't have to perform for your value. You can rest in the knowledge that you are already valuable.

Everyone says they want to align with the core values of ease, but they delay doing so until retirement. If you want to align to ease now, you'll have to first allow a season of rest so that your body can literally change over. Your whole chemical makeup is built around denying your feelings and taking manic action. Your body needs to turn over like the ocean turns over or the snake sheds its skin.

So many of my clients want rest and ease. They've been going upstream; now they want to go downstream. They want the flow of life to take them now. They're in a mature enough place to realize that the flow of life can take them to a far better place.

But there's a reason people don't rest. It's because it's excruciating. Why is it excruciating to sit in ease? Because the moment they stop and rest, they have to deal with what's really there.

Ease sounds great, but ease isn't the easy way out. It's easier for an older person to die after they retire than it is to deal with their emotions, and many people stay in whatever state they're in throughout their lives because they don't want to go through the phase of rest.

THE LAW OF LEAST EFFORT

When someone tells me they're busy, running around like a chicken with their head cut off, I know that person is not full. Not only can that person not be trusted, but they're also not tapping into one of the greatest laws that governs our universe: *the law of least effort*.

This law of the universe says that the least produces the most. Opposite this law is manic action, which produces *dis-creation*. Dis-creation happens when you are over-producing—tilling up the ground and the seed and never allowing what you have planted to take root.

When you tap into the law of the universe, you tap into the law of least effort. It's like a Bruce Lee punch—most efficient and powerful. The small seed produces the biggest plant.

Many people work much more than I do, but I make in an hour what they make in a month. Why is that? It's not effort-based. If effort determines abundance, a lot of people would be making a lot more money.

Most people think rest would be nice, but they aren't sure how they'll pay their bills. They fear they won't make money if they choose rest. This is where the law of least effort kicks in! It's all about tapping into what is most potent, which will look different for each person...but you can't fake it. The thing that is most potent is usually what you've been giving away for free.

In my case, I compare my coaching with my role as a

pastor. When I was a pastor, I was meeting with people all the time, coaching them up. But I didn't get paid for that. I didn't know I could get paid for what came the easiest. Now I work 6-8 hours a week doing what I love, getting paid in a month what I got paid in a year as a pastor.

Are you giving away what is most potent and charging for what is the hardest? If so, it will be difficult to make this switch. It won't feel normal at first. But if you're following along with what I'm saying, you have to be willing to feel uncomfortable feelings to move through this process and receive all the rewards. Stop tilling the ground. Start harvesting!

THE NEED TO BE PRODUCTIVE

Remember that we talked about the three ways we protect ourselves from emotional pain:

1. **I am what others think of me.**
2. **I am what I do or my production.**
3. **I am what I have.**

Let's focus for a moment on that second protective mechanism: production. No matter what family you grew up with or what personality you have, the basic message many of us constantly received was, you are your production. You are what you do. But your existence in life is really about how you feel. If you're feeling good, life is great. And to feel great, you have to go through this process of ease and allowance, allowing the weeds to emerge.

In my case, I can't sit still. I've got to be doing something. I've got to be productive. That need to be productive was built into me from a young age, plus it's just part of my personality.

If you're like me, what happens when you just need to rest or there's nothing to do? Maybe you create problems to solve. In other words, you sabotage yourself, your business, the happiness to solve the problem. It's easier to create drama and try to solve it than deal with the drama inside of us.

Of course, drama takes on many forms. Some people spend most of their time in the doctor's office. Others binge watch Netflix to escape. Still others watch the news all the time because they're addicted to the endless cycles of drama.

For me, the pressure to produce and to maintain a high level of drama manifested in my body as an orange-sized tumor in my colon that had to be taken out. You could even see in my belly the result of all the emotional trauma I tried to run from. The dis-ease for me became a tumor, because dis-ease becomes disease.

Now, I must get a colonoscopy every two years to monitor my health because all of that stored energy collects in my stomach. Just another reason to be even more proactive in making sure my emotions are not getting stuck.

The tumor showed up when I started into a season of rest. When you finally rest, it all comes to the surface. You take away that protective layer of manipulation, control, or denial, and you get to see where you really are.

LIVING FROM REST, NOT PRESSURE

The tough part about rest is that things will look worse before they get better. Choosing ease is really intense. So often, vacations are big attempts to decompress, which means we start in a place of pressure, not rest.

Once, my wife and I were in Las Vegas, and it was the third day when it literally hit me: "Oh my gosh," I said, "we're either going to a strip club or I'm doing cocaine. I'm going off the rails here. I'm going to spend every dime we have, and I'm going to put it on red. Either that, or I have to sit out here by the pool and feel my feelings." It was that intense.

I chose to feel it. I released so much energy and was finally able to be connected.

For one of the first times, I stayed within, and it felt like a wrestling match with myself. Since doing this, I have trademarked the 4 As process that I used. I laid next to the pool in the long pool chair, with a towel over my head. First, I became highly *aware* of what was happening inside of me. I *accepted* all the disturbed internal energy that was active.

I squirmed in that chair like I did when I was ten years old and I was in a boring church service. I could finally feel all that was going on. So, I began to *amplify* an intense energy that was in my chest. I stayed with it and did not leave that chair until the energy resolved. After the emotions resolved, they led to *action*. I had one of the most connective and passionate nights with Ginny in our entire marriage.

I have experienced a similar process of feeling pressure when visiting family. Our families are a lot like fish. After three days, it goes bad. You have to either talk about what's real or get the hell out of there.

Eventually, I realized I needed to start speaking up with my family at the beginning of vacations. I started the process early so I could have time with them in that space of connection.

After vacations, most people take another three to seven days to decompress.

But can we be successful without the pressure? Can we go into vacation from a state of rest? Can we leave from vacation with that same rest? We all know how to decompress from pressure, but we don't know how to ever rest.

If you've been around someone who lives in pressure, everything means so much—the deal, the money. But people who live from rest have a baseline of trust. They feel if you do the deal, you do the deal. If you don't, you don't, but they're good either way.

Rest is like the cobra; the cobra is waiting in the grass for just the right time to strike; it's not taking manic action. It waits and waits and then, in the right moment, it strikes and kills. That's rest. Waiting patiently and then, **BOOM**, the inspired action happens and desires are fulfilled.

People are attracted to people who live from rest. I recently did a massive deal from a place of rest, and the person couldn't get enough of my energy. I could have just named the price because they didn't know why they wanted this. All they knew was that they wanted to be in the energy.

FEELING IS HEALING

At one of my seminars, I had a client show up looking like he'd been hit over the head. His hair was combed to one side. He was slumped over; he looked terrible.

He had eight successful businesses all over the United States. I found out he was in the midst of building one of his big businesses. To do it, he bypassed himself. Now divorced, he was drinking heavily, tilling up the ground, so to speak. Religion wasn't doing it for him either. Nothing outside of himself was working.

We had to bring him back to himself. In his case, he had to put his gift and his role behind his back for a season and be willing to rest, so that he could get to his heart. He was right here, at this phase.

Leading with your heart can sometimes be messy.

When you lead with your heart, you must choose to rest. Otherwise, you will go through sabotaging of yourself and others in some form. If your wife leaves you, or your business shuts down and you go bankrupt, or your kid ends up in drug rehab, you're going to feel that, too.

It's much easier to bring on this deconstruction yourself than for the universe to bring it on. I was reminded of this when I watched a controlled implosion of the Kingdome stadium in Seattle. I thought, *What if the Kingdome fell because of an earthquake while thousands of people were in it?* With a controlled deconstruction, there are far fewer casualties. It's much better to have a few messy conversations with your spouse than to look up one day and find out he or she wants a divorce. You will feel both times, but one comes with interest.

What's amazing, though, is that feeling is healing, and we can transfer feelings into positive energy.

CHAPTER 10

The Art of Transmutation: Your Inner Ninja Turtle

Now, the shifting and sorting of your world is happening. There's real white space. The old is leaving, but the new had not come in yet.

You're still in the season of rest with not much going on. Things haven't fully turned over. You're just in this white space, and that's when people get scared.

If you don't have a white space, you can't create a masterpiece, but it's scary—that emptiness, the blankness filled with, "Oh, I should be doing something. I should be producing." There's something beautiful about having a season where there's nothing going on. Again, the outflow is happening, and the inflow hasn't quite come yet.

This is where we are confronting the old BS (belief systems). We're addressing the belief that we're missing out and falling behind if we don't produce for value. That BS is getting dealt with here.

A lot of ancient texts call this place the void. Creation comes out of the void.

The Bible says, "Darkness fell upon the face of the deep." Out of that void, all of life was created. There's nothing more powerful than seeing someone get proactive about their healing and then bring their life to that place of simplicity, so they can build what they really want from that one seed. How powerful, right? How potent?!

My wife and I did that with our house. It was an amazing house, but we didn't love it. We went through the process of purging all the way down, from our house, to our business, to everything.

We kept only what we loved. We weren't left with much. I didn't know I loved so little and liked so much.

STOP ATTRACTING LOWER ENERGIES

When we don't feel safe within ourselves, we attract people with lower energies to keep us safe and grounded. Big fish in a small pond syndrome. This keeps us from moving forward in this process. We remain with the lower energies because we've found some form of false groundedness there.

You end up attracting a lot of controllers to your life who operate through the lower energies of guilt and shame. Then we use guilt and shame to keep us falsely safe. We're afraid we are going to mess it all up, so we put a bunch of people around us to control us. We become imprisoned in our own businesses.

I coached an executive who had a lot of unprocessed negative energy. He was hiding his pain behind his impenetrable optimism. In turn, he attracted people to him who were also negative.

My client turned it around by connecting to how he really feels. He realized that avoiding his feelings was keeping him playing way lower than what he was created for. He'd attracted a bunch of sixes and sevens rather than nines and tens. Nines and tens cause him to feel because of their elevated state. He could remain hidden with sixes and sevens.

If you have people around you who feel like they need to protect you, that's a sign that you are not willing to protect yourself, and you've built a co-dependent culture. When my client realized what was happening, he elevated into how he wanted to live and began to surround himself with the people he wanted to attract into his life.

NEGATIVE ENERGIES TO POSITIVE POWER

In the book *Think and Grow Rich*, Napoleon Hill talks about the power of transmutation, specifically transmuting sexual energy into focus and power. For some reason, this is something none of us are ever taught.

The fact is that all these negative energies from the second down are actually great reserves of power. But how do we transmute our lower emotions into greater clarity for what we really want? How do we transform the dormant power in these traumas from something that is hurting us to a positive? It's time to transmute them into massive inspired action, clarity, and energy.

This is where you want to use the 4 As: **awareness, acceptance, amplify, action**.

Using this process, you'll take your lower energies and turn them into decision-making power. And once you decide, the whole universe conspires to make it happen.

But it's intense to hold these negative energies and flow them all the way to clarity, and ultimately to take inspired action. In many ways, it's a similar process to holding your sexual energy.

AN EMOTIONAL AFFAIR

My wife and I have been together since I was seventeen. When we were twenty-four, she was pregnant, and I wasn't getting the connection I wanted. Marriage wasn't fixing me. I didn't know how to be with myself, or what was going on inside of me. I didn't know how to give myself love, and I definitely didn't know how to transmute my painful emotions into love and connection with my wife.

I wanted connection and I wasn't getting it. Like so many people do, I tried to look outside for connection rather than give it to myself. I want you to really hear this. What you are trying to get from your spouse is what you will learn to give to yourself.

What happens the moment you feel disconnection? You feel the lower energies of loneliness or even abandonment instead of the higher energies of love and connection.

We're taught that we go outside to fix it, or we demonize the person and blame all the way to separation. I had the choice to take that path, or to take the internal path of awareness—the path that leads to radical acceptance. Thankfully, I chose the latter.

The most loving thing you can do for yourself is to accept those energies slowly and fully. And then there's a new step, called *amplify*. You amplify that energy rather than abandon it, and this is where the beauty of this process emerges in full effect.

Have you ever considered amplifying the abandonment you feel inside and going with it? What would happen if you amplified that energy? I'll tell you what it would do. It would create resolution.

You might have to yell or shake or take a massive breath. But from that place, there's an opening, and you'll feel a peace and understanding beyond the mind. When you tap into that peace, that collective mainframe that we all have access to, that's where the inspired action and the creative power is.

You gain clarity; you know what to do. And you have the rocket fuel to decide on what you want and take massive action to make it happen.

In my case, I knew that I didn't want to have an affair. I knew I was called to be with my wife. I could finally see what she was going through. I channeled all that energy toward her, and she reciprocated physically.

Instead of emotionally masturbating out my energies, my energy went exactly where I wanted it to go, and there was an increase in care, nurture, and connection.

PRUNING THE BRANCH

This final part of the down process is like pruning the branch. Very few are willing to prune the branch because they're afraid it won't grow back.

Many people spend the early part of their life figuring out, testing, experimenting, before they have something to prune. There's a difference between the purifying fires burning away dead branches and the pruning back of a live branch.

In this process, you find that one branch that's been producing fruit.

You get to see the one thing that you love. If all the dead branches are gone and you're asked to still prune back the one branch that actually has fruit on it, that takes a lot of trust.

This is the moment of great power; all the dead branches

have fallen away, and you are left with the decision to prune the one branch that is bearing fruit. You've got this. Don't stop. The harvest is on its way.

In West Texas where my wife and I first started out, we had very few trees. I pruned back the one tree we had, and Ginny got so mad at me. She loves trees so much and thought I'd killed the tree. But when spring came, it was the most magnificent, beautiful thing we'd ever seen. It came back three times bigger than what it was before.

We always go back to that tree because it represents so much. It represents the point just before our great elevation.

PHASE THREE

———

UP

———

CHAPTER 11

The Vision Emerges

Vision is a function of an awakened heart, just as sight is a function of the eyes.

You've allowed everything that doesn't serve you in this season to fall away. You let it all burn away. Now you're left with just your heart.

You're starting to see big things again. Reawakening, reemergence of passion—these are all present in this part of the process.

This is a season of transformation, a marked change in physical appearance. You begin to know you've changed; others notice as well. Paul talked about this kind of transformation in his prayer to the Ephesians. He wrote, "I pray that the *eyes of your heart may be enlight-*

ened in order that you may know the hope to which you are called."

TIME FOR AN UPGRADE

Four years ago, I stopped everything that I did not love. I let go of the parts of my thriving company that weren't GREAT! From my team, to my clients, to the opportunities that weren't in my highest alignment. It was time for a new vision to emerge, time for an upgrade. I'm experiencing the physical manifestation of that upgrade right now.

The business was good. I had already discovered my fruit-bearing branch, but it still needed to be pruned for a new season, so that it could be even more of what I wanted.

Pruning began at the end of the last phase, but it's important to continue pruning, too. If you've ever been around trees, you understand the importance of pruning. I grew up in a town where once there was a pecan orchard. If the branches weren't pruned, I could always tell. Everything would just look gnarly. The branches would start falling everywhere, and the trees wouldn't produce fruit.

If you are willing to keep pruning, you'll experience a true upgrade. This requires a lot of trust and courage. "If I cut off this branch, will it grow back and produce even more fruit?" This is where you get to learn how to trust your heart, how to trust God, and how to trust the laws of the universe.

If you don't trust that your heart can come through for you, less will always mean less. If your identity is your company, you're not going to let go of it. You won't let go of your spectacular house because to you that feels like losing value.

When I knew I needed an upgrade, I gave away a lot of amazing stuff. But I also got to a blank canvas, where I could let the power of my imagination do its work. The law of vision states that what you **SEE** with your awakened heart is what you will reproduce. What you see with your imagination, consistently, will surely come to pass.

If you want to go global with your business or take anything in your life to another level, you have to be willing to let go of the weight. You must be willing to let go physically, but you also have to be able to let go mentally and emotionally.

MOVING FROM TALK TO INSPIRED ACTION

Many people talk about letting go of fear and stepping into their vision or moving into the mindset of abundance, but you have to actually live it out. You have to go through the intense work of the first two downs. And you have to be willing to keep pruning.

Are you willing to allow yourself to feel? Great! Now are you willing to take inspired action on behalf of your vision? It doesn't just happen on its own.

Remember that 'response ability' is the ability to respond? It's time to step up that ability one more notch here. It's time to give to yourself what you've been giving to others. It's time to take inspired action for that upgrade.

As we move up, as we upgrade our lives, each individual breaststroke should be determined by the questions:

1. What am I feeling?
2. What do I want?
3. What am I willing to do about it?

If you're tuned in, you'll know *what you feel*. If you feel frustrated, feel it. Remember the four As. Never try to take action before you feel and flow your emotional energy. That will only discreate what you really want and lead to manic action. Once you feel internally clear, now it's time to ask, *What do I want?*

Ask yourself: "What do I really want?" It may come out like, "I just want to feel free."

Okay, you want freedom? What feels like freedom to you?

You want financial abundance? Okay, own that. Don't shy away from it.

What does financial abundance mean?

You're tired of making X amount; you really want half a million dollars?

Okay, feel that frustration and use the feelings to create greater clarity around what you want. Your frustrated feelings are fuel for clarity.

Now that you feel it, now that you know what you want, you can move to inspired action.

What are you willing to do about it?

Boom, the answer comes. Call that person right now. Follow the lead and call. They might say no, but there's a greater chance of them saying yes when you're in this energy. Maybe the lead tells you to call your mom, and your mom says, "Uncle Larry died and left you half a million bucks." That literally happened for us when Ginny's granddad died.

When you're tuned in—when you tap into that emotional energy—anything can happen.

THE IMPULSES OF THE HEART

To take inspired action, you have to start listening to what's going on inside of you, what I call impulses of the heart.

Follow the impulse.

When you do, the world starts to come to you. People feel your difference and want to be around it. They don't know why, but they like your difference and want to associate with you.

Keep listening.

At this stage, I see many of my clients go from micro-managing their companies and their lives to being truly visionary, inspirational leaders. They can do more even when they're doing less. They can truly adopt the *heart over hustle* lifestyle.

There is an adjustment period here. You start to do less and produce far more. You tap into the power of the heart. You experience the power of inspired action as far greater than the manic action you have been operating in.

The law of least effort states that the least produces the most. The smallest, most potent seed produces the biggest plant.

This requires adjusting because you are used to proving your value by being busy. Now you are not in your busyness but are instead making inspired moves from above your busyness. This is the power of vision.

CHAPTER 12

Heart Over Hustle

There is a hustle movement, a grind movement happening right now in the world of business and entrepreneurship. Of course, there's a measure of results that way of life can produce, but it comes at a really high cost.

Then there's heart—the living *from*, not *for* reality. With the heart, you literally tap into an energy that's a thousand times greater than manic action. Some tests say it's 5,000 times greater, electromagnetically speaking.

When you live by the heart, you know you're too valuable to constantly have to hustle. And this isn't about entitlement. It's about trust. You're going to wait for the bigger, more aligned, opportunity to emerge. You are willing to hold the line and hold the value. That's a powerful place to be.

What can you do from a place of that feeling of integrity? It really sets the new tone for your life. You win every time when you take a stand for your heart.

"WHAT DO I WANT?"

For me, the change from hustle to heart was obvious because I went from sixty hours a week to six at the max. I went from a $60,000 salary to $600,000. My hours decreased, but my level of influence increased. I went from working with people in small-town Texas to working with executives, professional athletes, entertainers, and CEOs from all over the world.

What did I do to live from the heart? I stopped doing things out of obligation. I asked, *What do I really want?* And I was willing to be honest with myself about the answer.

It's often only in hindsight that we can see how the hustle we had before was rooted in fear, a lack of feeling protected and provided for. When we start protecting and providing for ourselves internally, we finally see what was waiting to emerge: quantum, exponential results.

THE HEART IS SMART

The heart is smart, and you'll discover that when you let go of figuring it out and just following the impulse. The more you try to figure it out, the worse it gets. You start to discreate what you really want.

It's easy to get off course. Society is telling you to do more and work harder. Produce, produce, produce so that you can be somebody. This is where it starts to get really heavy; that heaviness is a signpost telling you that you are going in the wrong direction. The moment it gets heavy, go back up. Get back up into the feeling, into the energy.

When you listen to your heart, it will tell you what to do. I have seen this time and time again—in my own life and the lives of those I surround myself with.

I recently met with someone worth $300 million for breakfast. In that moment, my heart told me it was the right time to suggest a partnership. I hadn't been ready before. We'd just been growing a friendship, then boom! My heart said it was time to partner. I owned it. I took inspired action and ended that day $120,000 richer.

Also keep an eye out for when you move back to manic action. You'll know you've moved back that direction if you feel you're constantly looking *for* approval, love, connection outside of yourself. You'll notice that you don't feel connected to your heart and actually feel afraid.

The heart leads to feeling connected to yourself and

deeply inspired; hustle leaves you disconnected from yourself and depleted. It's that simple.

UNEXPECTED SOURCES

As you listen to your heart, inspiration will sometimes show up in the strangest places.

Stay ready. Be alert. The heart's message could be small.

I remember one time feeling I was supposed to go to a particular restaurant in LA. I went there and ran into this guy who is one of the biggest lawyers in LA.

I worked with a CEO who took inspired action to have a new location. What was remarkable was the source of his idea.

All he knew was that he wanted to take his daughter to lunch one day. There at the table with his daughter and her classmates, one of the girls said something that sparked the idea of a new location.

The girl had no idea what her words meant to him. He wasn't expecting anything particular from the lunch, but he was ready with new ears to hear. It turned out that finding his company a new location increased his net worth by $10 million.

Unexpected sources of inspiration will affect more than just your money; they will show up in every area of your life.

One random Tuesday I was struggling with IBS-type symptoms mixed with emotional tension. So I decided not to avoid it but instead tune into the wisdom of my body—especially to the painful sensations and frustrated emotions that were showing up inside of me.

After I took time to feel, I heard, *Take a walk*. So I started walking and listening. I took it easy and gave myself a lot of love. I ended up at a local super-healthy restaurant that had recently opened. As I was in line, I felt another nudge. *Buy that bread*. It was a $12 loaf of bread. Yes, $12.

I knew the bread was specially made for people who have gluten intolerance, but the middle-class mindset I had adopted in my childhood did not like that price one bit. I got up to the counter and squinted my eyes with a painful grimace. I ordered that damn bread.

Here's where this story gets really good. A lady standing behind said, "I've been wanting to try that bread but haven't yet. Let me know how it tastes." As she and her husband ordered, I opened up the loaf and grabbed a couple of extra plates. As they walked back my way, I invited them to try it with me. They were reluctant, but I insisted. They didn't want to eat all of my $12 loaf.

As we sat there breaking bread together, we introduced ourselves. When the man said his name, my eyes widened. I said, "Excuse me, did you say Dr. Bush?"

He said, "Yes, I'm Dr. Bush."

Then it hit me. The voice did sound familiar. Just an hour before arriving at the restaurant, I had been listening to him talk on a podcast. Ginny had heard Dr. Bush was a leading mind on gut health and asked me to listen to him.

So here I was, breaking gluten-free bread with Dr. Bush, at a random health food restaurant in California. What made the situation even more unpredictable was that the couple had just moved near us all the way from Virginia.

We continued chatting, and he gave me some amazing advice. Just as importantly, I was reminded of the power of following how you feel and taking inspired action on behalf of your heart. I literally listened to my gut, and it took me exactly where I needed to go.

As you experience life with new ears to hear, you will be able to move into your own genius alignment.

CHAPTER 13

———

Genius Alignment

We grow up with an idea that the hardest work demands the most value. I learned to hustle from a young age. I knew that when I did, I would receive approval. Because I hustled, my tennis coaches praised me and would tell the country club kids to "play more like Brandon."

It makes sense that we spend most of our time aligning to what is difficult because that is what we've equated with value. We've lived by the hustle and grind mindset.

But genius alignment works the opposite way. When we live from this new mindset, we believe that *what comes easiest demands the most value.* For most people, genius alignment feels wrong. If you were taught for your whole life that what is most difficult is most valuable, what do you do with genius, which comes the easiest?

The problem is that so many people give what comes the easiest away for free, and it never gets truly compensated. In the church world, people give away their genius all the time. If they're a teacher and love teaching, they go to church to teach Sunday school and give away their genius for free wherever they can. To make matters worse, they then spend the rest of the week doing what's hard for them to do.

Genius alignment is about doing what you're a ten at, not what you've trained yourself to be a seven or eight at. Gay Hendricks, author of *The Big Leap* and world-renowned coach, explains that there's a big difference between your *zone of genius* and your *zone of competence*. People think they have to do the other stuff to be provided for and be protected, and I'm telling you no, you don't.

DESERVING EASE

If you have children, you've probably had the experience of seeing your child asleep and thinking they are so beautiful. You go in their room and look at them. All you can say is, "Oh, my God." That's the energy I'm asking you to get back to here. It's the transfer of love—pure, unconditional love. We give this to our children so easily when they are asleep, but we can't give it to ourselves.

In a perform-for-value society, in a *how many steps have*

you taken society, it's not easy to get back to the basics. It's hard to see the great value of a sleeping child. That's where your greatest value is, too—**in your greatest state of rest and flow.**

This is where we start to build into the you that is beyond the performance, beyond right and wrong. As Rumi says, "Beyond right and wrong, there is a field."

When the value is you, you're breaking culture. And when you've aligned to your genius, you must stand for reciprocal exchange. No one else can stand for you; you must stand for yourself.

Then the world will want more of what you have. That's how it works. Your world will recalibrate to that alignment.

We train the world how to treat us, just as we train our kids and customers how to treat us. If I wanted to charge $1 million for what I do, and I stayed aligned to that long enough, I have no doubt it would happen.

If you fudge on yourself and the numbers, the world's going to fudge back on you. But if you hold the line for a reciprocal exchange of values, even though it may take six months or a year, it will happen. It is law.

REALIZE YOUR GIFTS

Sometimes you'll need to go through a few stages of life to see your gifts more clearly, but if you're reading this book you probably already have a solid idea of what you're great at.

Take someone who is great at getting tasks accomplished. They truly find joy in handling all the details. Why are we trying to make them an entrepreneur? They would be terrible at it, and they would hate it. That person could be a number two, three, or four somewhere and dominate. If they're number four at a company that's worth $300 million, they'll be making $400,000 a year doing something they love. Plus, they'll have tons of ownership.

You may love working sixty hours a week to get a lot accomplished, so do it. Go for it. Or you may want to work only four hours and hit it big—do that.

Do and be exactly who you are, and let the chips fall where they may. You might balk at that statement. It might sound too risky. But isn't it riskier to live your whole life miserable?

When you live *for* protection and provision, you do what you hate. When you live *from* provision and protection, you align to your genius.

BEYOND GIFTS

We live best in genius alignment when there is a convergence of gifting, calling, and embodiment (which is when the universe and others recognize we have arrived). It's one thing to have the gift and another to have a life calling and to embody that calling. That is when we experience true congruence.

Maybe you have a gift to draw, but is it your life calling to be an artist? Gifting and calling can lead you to your purpose. Then there is a final stage to the process in which the world responds, "Oh yeah, that's what this person was put on the planet to do." I refer to that as anointing; you could use a different word. The point is that when these three come together, they reveal your full genius.

When these three converge and you decide to follow the genius within, there will be certain barriers or programming you will have to hurdle. You'll think, *This is so easy. Why should I get paid to do it?*

There has to be a shift that what you could do in your sleep is what should demand the most value. That's a huge pivot point for some people.

RECOGNIZE WHAT TO LET GO OF

We experience the reality of what we were put on the

planet to do at different times in different ways. With greater realization of our genius comes greater release of what isn't fully aligned. I feel like I was put on the planet to use my voice—to coach others and to speak in front of people. This comes so naturally to me, and I love it.

But at one point I felt like I needed to be a great counselor, too. I felt I needed to really help people with their issues and do deep trauma work. But I'm only a seven at that kind of work, not a ten. Counseling someone through their issues does not come naturally to me. I excel at shifting people's perspective, and I love embodying and communicating these radical ideas.

So, I had to let go of everything that didn't align to shifting others' perspective through my experiential knowledge. When I try to do the other stuff, that's when it gets heavy for me.

RECIPROCAL EXCHANGE OF VALUE

It's one thing to connect to your genius; it's another thing to have reciprocal exchange of value for your genius. At church, I was giving my genius but was not getting a reciprocal exchange. I provided priceless value to people without getting paid. That was my fault. It's up to me to quantify priceless.

There are a lot of starving artists and musicians out there. Why? They have the gift, the calling, and others acknowledge these as well. In fact, others literally cheer them on. But they still end up prostituting themselves out. They have a mentality of lack within their world. And everyone keeps telling them, "That's just how it is." In the end, they believe that they have to live poor.

Do you receive a reciprocal exchange of value in all areas of your life—friendships, relationships, work? Or are you settling for far less? If you are giving more than what you're receiving, shame on you. You would rather be victimized than stand up for yourself. When I charge my clients for what I do, that protects our connection because I feel valued. Otherwise, the connection is eroded, and the exchange becomes a mere transaction.

LETTING GO OF CONTROL

The main reason people do not align to their geniuses is because they are taking control of the details. They are controlling that lesser version of themselves. To move from general manager to inspired leader, or to move from $60,000 to $600,000, you have to release control.

To not have to control how other people think or what other people do, you will have to feel those uncomfortable feelings down in the lower belly. That is where feelings of control hang out. That's where disappointment, shame, and guilt are found. **They can keep you forever in cycles of limitation.**

Why doesn't everyone play at ten? Because not everyone is willing to deal with the uncomfortable energies inside of themselves. When you're playing at a high level, those low energies can't be in the same field. So they're going to have to be resolved.

To stay in that inspired leader role, you not only have to hold your ground, but you have to allow everyone around you to process what's really going on. This can be tough in the beginning. It will feel like chaos. A little hell in the hallway. But ultimately, you and those around you will experience an infusion of energy that produces opportunity for those who want to take it. Chaos will give way to divine order.

For those who step into that real place of being a ten, they will get paid to be a ten.

Now, you've created a culture and container for honest conversation. Now, you live in a beautifully connected environment. Now, everyone is operating in their genius.

One of my clients went through this stage of the process and went from one struggling store to owning stores nationwide. He now has a booming business because of the sifting and sorting and the genius alignment for him and all those around him. Things were a little shaky with the initiation of this new way, but then boom, exponential growth!

When you aren't willing to let go of control in any area of your life, you will experience frustration, and at some point that frustration will start to emerge. This happens all the time in marriages. What's been bubbling under the surface for years finally comes out. That's the point when it's tempting to go back to managing. If the couple is willing to ride through the chaos, they will experience the beauty of truth and freedom on the other side.

You can see that things might seem to get "worse" before transformation comes. But the reality is they aren't getting worse; they're just getting real. Reality—rather than denial—gives way to connection and freedom.

LIMITING BS (BELIEF SYSTEMS)

Many people also have to break through mental constructs—programming that tells them, "Money doesn't grow on trees." To shift this kind of BS, I like to go from the emotion back to the belief. The emotion is a signpost to the limiting belief.

Start with the emotion. The emotion allows you to recognize that the belief doesn't serve you anymore. It's in opposition to your highest self.

So many people try to fix themselves—at church or otherwise—through mental conceptualization and behavior modification. That methodology never solves the problem. The feeling is the bigger energy. That feeling can be an amazing illuminator and break up the limiting belief.

I have so much success in creating true transformation because I follow the E-motion. If you're thinking about genius alignment but have a knot in your stomach around money, don't stop there. Follow the knot and see what it reveals. Maybe the knot reveals that your dad said to not ever be like that rich person or to ever go bankrupt. The emotion reveals why you don't ever take chances with money. Your dad's fear turned into a mental construct, and that mental construct was transferred to you. But it will show up most clearly when you pay attention to the emotion.

Imagine how you could move into your genius alignment if you could overcome these mental constructs. Not only will you be able to do what you love in life, but you will feel a hell of a lot more connected as well.

CHAPTER 14

The Five Steps of Creating Connection

As we keep moving up and aligning to our genius, we want to also make sure we are creating connection in every area of life. The five steps of creating connection can help us here.

These steps are tools of awareness. They allow you to realize when you're not being authentic or connected to your heart.

1. **You realize you are not being yourself.** Here's that feeling you get when you recognize how fake you're being (disgust). That plastic smile that hurts your face.

You've been faking it for far too long. It's over. No more. You are taking your power back.

2. **You allow yourself to process your emotions without any filter.** We often won't process our feelings because it feels dishonoring. We don't want it to look messy. This is the season to get it all out. Own whatever you feel.

3. **You realize you not being yourself and that you not being connected has affected others.** This is where you feel real remorse for the hurtful choices that have come out of disconnection. Some people try to jump into "please forgive me" (stage three) before they have truly allowed themselves to feel deeply. This person understands the concepts of connection but does not experience true resolution. They feel a martyrdom syndrome but never process their own trauma. They've taken on false humility, which is pride and unprocessed pain. Only step into stage three if you have given yourself full permission to process and express your pain.

4. **You start to become vulnerable with your inner circle.** Vulnerability needs to be a way of life with your inner circle. Some will leave because that's too much for them, but with others you'll build lifelong bonds.

5. **Relational accountability happens here.** This is not control; this is you allowing yourself to be held accountable to your greatness, and you allow others

to see you. When you do this within a business, you no longer have to control your employees. You hold them accountable to their greatness. That's a whole different way of operating a business. You start to treat your employees, and even your family, at a different level of consciousness. Accountability is not about behavior but calling. When you treat people according to who they truly are, they respond. When a teacher treats a student not for how they're behaving but who they really are, they become who the teacher treats them as. If the teacher treats them like a problem child, they will be a problem child. If the teacher views them as highly gifted, the child's gifts rise to the surface.

MY TED TALK

What does this awareness and connection look like in real life?

I did a TED talk where I spoke on heart over hustle. Going in, I knew I was either going to give the mental concepts of vulnerability with a bit of feeling behind it, or I was going to be vulnerable and give the experience and transmission of vulnerability.

Being my higher self is being a transmitter, not a polished speaker. But that feels vulnerable. After all, the polished speaker has protected me. The transmitter is pretty raw. It brings on a much faster energy that is not as controllable.

I knew that I could either clear this energy and give the concepts, or I could take all the emotions I was feeling to the stage.

When you're making this sort of shift, you are going through what transformation leader Bob Proctor calls a terror barrier. It's actually a revealer that you're elevating your consciousness.

I decided to take that terror to the stage. I rooted in it, and that led to one of the most amazing moments of my life. By the time I finished, there wasn't a dry eye in the crowd. I received a five-minute standing ovation. My parents came onstage, and the whole crowd came forward and gathered around us. That kind of thing was unheard of at that event.

What happened? I allowed myself to be open and to not shun my emotions. Right from the beginning, I was crying; I allowed the audience in. I was deeply connected within myself and it overflowed into a deep connection with my dad from the stage. He got to stand in for fathers everywhere, which was so beautiful.

I didn't bow to the emotional tension of the moment. I

owned myself. Even friends who weren't there asked why my presentation wasn't more polished. Some thought I missed a real opportunity. These kinds of experiences of full-on connection always come with some misunderstanding.

But for me, I proved to myself that I can't be bought. I didn't just talk about my message; I embodied it on a big stage for myself, a stage I had wanted to be on for a long time.

I felt honest and trustworthy. I felt congruent. I came through for me, not everyone else. When you come through for you, that's integrity. And in turn, that room felt like I stood for them and their heart. When we come through for ourselves, we come through for those around us.

RENTING FRIENDS

A client of mine had an important moment of decision like I did. He had hired his friend, as so many people do, because he didn't want to deal with his aloneness. But eventually, he had to be honest with himself and his friend about the origination of their business relationship. The truth was that he rented his friend so that he didn't have to deal with his feelings. The friend was not actually the right business partner for him.

Through our work together he learned how to befriend himself. He no longer needed to rent his friends to escape having to feel. Making the decision to fire his friend was one of the hardest things he'd ever done. He didn't know if their friendship would survive the honesty. Still, he chose to ride the energy and not abort because of the terror he felt. He was honest, vulnerable, and clear in what he wanted. And extremely brave.

In the end, his decision turned into elevation and expansion. He was actually able to upgrade his relationship with his friend and create a more meaningful partnership with him.

YOUR MOMENT OF DECISION

These examples illustrate the concept of a decision point. Before I went onstage, I had a moment of decision. Before my client had the conversation with his friend, he had a decision point.

The decision can produce connection and, therefore, big results. If you get consistent with making these decisions, you will live in a truly exponential reality. I call them "right turns." With our mental programming, the norm is a bunch of left turns, like a NASCAR track. We're constantly turning left to follow the track.

It's time to turn right.

My question for myself now is, how many right turns a day can I make? How often can I make a decision that goes beyond the mind?

Many people keep themselves safe in the Grey Zone of Indecision. It's a zone of protection but also great frustration—like purgatory, a manageable form of hell.

I am passionate about eradicating the Grey Zone because I know, from my own experience, that's how you produce quantum, divine results. That's how you become the city on the hill.

___

CHAPTER 15

The City on the Hill

You've changed. You've transformed. You're living life on a different energetic plane and you're a different person.

Physically speaking, our organs turn over every three or four months. You have literally shed your skin and you're completely new. The new you is emerging and evident to the world.

Now people come to see your beauty, and they want to be around it. They're drawn to the fast vibration of your illuminated heart.

You're set apart. You're the city on a hill that's bright.

You don't have to manipulate people anymore. You've shed that skin. You've done it; you're doing it. You've been brave. Now you're living from a whole new energy. It's not about hustling and grinding; it's about alignment and flow.

THE JOKE, THE THREAT, THE TEACHER

Before you can be the city on the hill, however, you have to face a season of owning yourself. When you go fully through this process, you will first be a joke.

And becoming a joke is a vital part of the process. If you're not a joke at some point, you've not gone through this process and transitioned. You're just talking about it and playing with it, sticking your toe in the water.

At some point in my journey, people said, "What happened to Brandon? He used to have it all together, and he just ruined it all. He squandered his inheritance." Before that point, I'd never been a joke. I'd always been the talented, gifted, handsome athlete. Externally, I had all the potential for success. Now suddenly it was, "Brandon is losing the church. It doesn't make any sense." People didn't know what to make of it.

In the wake of being seen as a joke, I had to feel what had always been there.

When you're a joke, your gift can't bail you out. It was illegal for me to give my gift in this season.

This is where you hold onto aloneness and rejection like they're your best friends. This is where you go in and find your power within yourself. You can't get it from anyone else. It's all about YOU. I think of the words of Jesus: "The Kingdom is in you." You've got to find that kingdom.

But when you look back at the joke season, you will see how beautiful it was. The people who stuck by you may be few, but the relationships were so deep and real.

Being the threat is also an essential stage along the way. Here, you start to become okay with yourself. You can't be bought, as I couldn't be bought when I did my TED Talk.

If we look at the totality of my life from zero to eighty or ninety, I'm probably just entering into threat stage. At a micro level, I've gone through this whole process, but on a macro level, I'm becoming a threat. I'm ready to be a force against the establishment. I've been through the joke season and stayed the course. I survived it and found myself. Along the way, I got a fire in my belly.

When people thought I was a joke, I gained 10,000 hours of expertise in my craft. Now I feel like I'm the best in the world at what I do, and no one can take that away from me. I no longer need to know others' opinion of me to feel valuable. I see and feel my own value.

Where some people used to wonder if I was okay, now they worry about me. Some say my path is damaging and not of God.

Each person deals with the threat stage in a different way. You might deal with it in a business setting or religious setting. When you rattle others' fear, they will try to put that on you. But people's projection of fear is a signpost that you're on the right track. Greatness or living from your genius will always threaten mediocrity. This season rattles the worlds of those who are too lazy or scared to transform. When you start to hear the rattles, you know you've started to threaten a way of life that has kept people safe.

Then after threat, you ultimately emerge as a teacher. You can now teach what you've walked through in the first two stages.

This part of the process is all about transmission. The greatest teachers are not polished. They often don't even have to be in the public eye. They just transmit an energy that you want to be around.

As a teacher, you feel true joy. I feel internally happy where I used to feel worried and full of anxiety.

But remember: **you can't selectively open.** We have to

open ourselves to all of it, and the final stage of vulnerability is real joy. When an entire family, organization, or culture has been fully through this process, they are totally comfortable with laughter and joy. This is when you know you've completed this transition.

When you become the teacher, you experience true play and ease. You're not pressured with time.

You also receive big results—an inheritance. You start to receive things you didn't work for. Other people plowed those fields and are bringing their crops to you. And vice versa.

I'm getting to a state where I want to do inheritance deals and partner with others so we can give each other stuff we didn't work for.

It's time to capitalize on leverage. You've already built value by going through this process, and value times leverage equals wealth. It's time to create true wealth in your life.

FROM ROBIN TO BATMAN

I once worked with a stay-at-home dad/uasi life coach/ philosopher. He experienced a major shift in the way he saw himself. He always saw himself as Robin, when he needed to see himself as Batman.

As we dove into his story, I related to him. I could see the ways he would need to go through the joke, threat, teacher phases. He was afraid of the aloneness and the rejection inside of himself. It caused him to stay in the grey zone of indecision. He was scared that his evolution would leave him disconnected from the ones he loved.

His dad was a pastor, and as a lot of PKs (pastor's kids) do, he saw himself as coming in second for his dad. In fact, the message he grew up with—first think of Jesus, then think of others, then think of yourself—was very damaging. He always felt like he was bad or wrong. When you feel second best, it's hard to break free from structures that no longer serve your highest good. He had to feel the emotions of guilt and shame. He had to feel all the feelings he had been avoiding.

Going through this process, he could see his goodness at the core. He broke through the religious paradigms of unworthiness, and as he did, he became Batman in the power of his own kingdom. This, of course, made him at first a joke to those around him. Eventually, he became a threat as others projected their fear onto him.

But then he emerged as a beacon. Today, he's a world-class coach and leader of men. He's a true master of the heart.

PARTNERING WITH THE FLOW OF LIFE

The word 'affluence' is derived from the word 'flow.' Now that you're here, at the end of this process, you are learning to partner with the flow of life.

Instead of going upstream, you're going downstream.

Sometimes that flow is at level one. You're in your inner tube and floating down the river with a drink in one hand. Then sometimes you're in a raft and it's level five. You're hitting big rapids, but you're not jumping out. You've embraced the flow of life. You've made a commitment that you'll stay in the raft and allow the flow of life to take you. That's where true partnership with the divine is, and that's what people are attracted to.

People now want to partner with and help you, and they genuinely mean it. They want to be in your field. They're tired of planting in infertile fields. They're tired of planting in guilt and shame structures. They're tired of tilling up the ground.

People come to me to be in my field all the time, because they know it's fertile. I do the same with others; I partner with them so I can be in their field and around their energy.

Recently, I partnered with a guy who comes from one of the wealthiest families in England. He's a Hollywood manager and very successful. He played a massive role in bigtime Hollywood projects. It's costing me ten percent of everything I make to partner with him. But I know he vibrates at a different field. He plays at a different level than I do, and I want access to that. I went to be in his field.

You must understand what kind of field you're partnering with because you will realize a LIKE return on your investment.

Conclusion

THE TRUE PIONEERS

You are a true pioneer. You're blazing a new trail for yourself and the world.

- **YOU have gone down below the role**—beyond identification with a name or with form. You've been brave and released your attachment to this identification.
- **YOU have continued down beyond the turbulent emotional pain.** You've stepped into real feeling—the frustration, the sadness, and the healing.
- **And now YOU are heading UP.** You're ready to launch from a connected space. And you actually have the rocket fuel you need to complete the journey.

The greatest thing you can do for the world is to accept

yourself fully and to accept your heart fully. As you resolve the violence, anger, frustration, and sadness within yourself, you partner with unity, oneness, and love.

By truly embodying this process, you become a true agent of transformation on the planet. The very personal victories you created have led to collective victories for everyone in your world. Your victories today are creating a beautiful future for yourself and generations to come.

We often think that things simply evolve, that it's all happenstance. The truth is that everything we see is a product of our own hearts and the energies that we transmit. The universe expands from us.

It's brave to open yourself to what is really going on inside of you. Reconnecting back to who you really are is the greatest of all outcomes. You were lost, and now you're found. You've come home to yourself, and it's time to celebrate!

It's courageous to pioneer through all the traumas and protective layers to get to that beautiful chocolatey center—your heart. To feel what you truly want to feel.

And it is all so worth it.

Now you can live your life *from* that place. Now you live

from fullness. You're playing with the house's money, and everything else is a bonus.

You are connected. You live from ease. You get massive results.

You have become an expert at **YOU**.

Acknowledgments

I want to include a note of thankfulness to the many teachers who have contributed to my life, teachers from many different backgrounds. You have added to my life beyond measure, and you have inspired much of what is shared in these pages. Thank you.

About the Author

Hailed by one of his CEO clients as "some sort of hybrid of Tony Robbins and Martin Luther King Jr," **BRANDON HAWK** helps people become experts at themselves and create the relationships, businesses, and lives they've always wanted but never knew were possible.

After joining the U.S. National Tennis team at the age of sixteen, Brandon had the opportunity to taste the double-edged sword of success at a young age. He retired from tennis after accomplishing his dream of playing in Wimbledon in his early twenties due to injury and began a 10-year journey of studying, developing, and testing principles of personal transformation, business growth, and human connection.

Brandon now works with executives and A-players who

pay $250,000/year or more to develop their capacity for a more quality, productive, and fulfilling life—all of whom credit Brandon with dramatic life change.

Beyond his personal coaching, Brandon is the creator of several programs and products that help people discover who they are and create lives they actually love living—including the YOU(TRAINING) event, YOU(COACHING) process, and the YOU(JOURNEY) workbook.

When not on the road speaking or working with his clients and their corporations, Brandon divides his time between introducing people to a better way of life, being with his beautiful wife—Ginny—and fathering his three fantastic kids—Austin, Conner, and Georgia.

Made in the USA
San Bernardino, CA
07 November 2019

59599953R00115